Praise for *Autobiography of a Face*

"Despite its unblinking stare at an excruciatingly painful subject, this is not a dour book. *Autobiography of a Face* is a book about image, about the tyranny of the image of a beautiful—or even pleasingly average—face. In the end, this tyranny is not so much overthrown as shrugged off."

—*New York Times Book Review*

"Written in a voice that is both compelling and insightful, *Autobiography of a Face* seems to mirror back to readers something relevant to their own lives....Despite the singular nature of her experience, Lucy Grealy manages to convince an amazing array of people that she is speaking directly to them."

—*Baltimore Sun*

"Grealy's calm, matter-of-fact manner, free of self-pity, heightens the horror and poignancy of her tale. She has undergone almost 30 operations to reconstruct her jaw, but the agonies of these procedures pale beside the anguish of being disfigured in a culture that so prizes physical beauty and perfection. She compensates—and ultimately overcomes—with wit, intelligence and an unconquerable spirit, all of which shine throughout this remarkable book."

—*Mademoiselle*

"Grealy's childhood recollections are vivid and true, as if in the writing of this book she was somehow able to inhabit her past. Though Grealy's experience was extraordinary, it is utterly affecting, for there is no one who has not felt the shame and self-doubt of physical inadequacy."

—*Elle*

"With fairy tale logic, as though to make up for her nearly unbearable fate, the gods also gave this young woman extraordinary gifts of perception and language. It is impossible to read *Autobiography of a Face* without having your consciousness raised forever."

—*Mirabella*

"Stunning. With only a one-in-twenty chance of survival, Grealy beat cancer, but this almost seemed inconsequential compared to the horrors of coping in a world that measures a woman's worth by her looks. Insightful and exquisitely written, this book reminds us that the things that makes us 'beautiful' are not always the things that other people see."

—*Seventeen*

"This harrowing, lyrical memoir is a striking meditation on the distorting effects of our culture's preoccupation with physical beauty."

—*Publishers Weekly* (starred)

"A gracefully written account of one woman's physical and spiritual struggle to surmount childhood cancer, permanent disfigurement, and, ultimately, 'the deep bottomless grief... called ugliness.' An unsentimental, honest, unflinching look at a single visage reflected (or distorted) in an unforgiving cultural mirror."

—*Kirkus Reviews*

"A memoir of disquieting candor and power. The account of Grealy's arduous coming of age is both haunting and inspirational, and she makes a lyrical statement about the complex relationship between beauty and self-worth in our society."

—*Ploughshares*

"[A] book that shares what it's like to be really different from other people....With exquisite prose and steely strength."

— *USA Today*

"This poet's ability to harness the pathos while transmuting her personal anguish into universal truths has enabled her to forge a powerful testament to the triumph of the human spirit."

— *Detroit Free Press*

"Grealy's is a book you want to hand people and say only, 'Read it.' As she describes her heroic efforts to transform her misfortune into a source of revelations about the beauty and mystery of life, we are humbled by her valor and the resiliency of her imagination. It's no surprise she is a tremendously powerful writer: she saved her own life by telling herself stories to live by. Now she'll change our lives by sharing them."

— *Booklist* (boxed)

"An astonishing book. To say that Grealy's memoir is the kind of work that can change lives may well be an understatement."

— *Santa Fe New Mexican*

"*Autobiography of a Face* is a memoir of great beauty. In her intensely elegant prose, Lucy Grealy describes the loneliness of pain, the confusion of childhood, the slow shock of her disfigured face with an exquisite unblinking intelligence that is both gracious and, improbably, filled with joy. I love this book."

— Cathleen Schine,
author of *Rameau's Niece*

"The majority of the world will find this book an incredible gift because of our feelings of ugliness and imperfection. Read it and free yourself to live a complete life free of the fear of rejection and filled with love and relationships. We are all scared but we can be healed. Read on."

—Bernie Siegel, M.D., author
of *Love Medicine, & Miracles*

"Autobiography of a Face is about that most wrenching of subjects—a child's suffering—but also moral courage, the hard battle of growing up and the unfolding of a writer's soul. An honest, deeply moving book."

—Eva Hoffman, author of
Lost in Translation and
Exit into Translation

Autobiography of a Face

LUCY GREALY

HARPER **PERENNIAL**

HARPER ● PERENNIAL

This book was published in 1994 by Houghton Mifflin Company. It is here reprinted by arrangement with Houghton Mifflin Company.

HarperCollins books may be purchased for educational, business, or sales promotional use. For information please write: Special Markets Department, HarperCollins Publishers Inc., 10 East 53rd Street, New York, NY 10022.

First HarperPerennial edition published 1995.

First Perennial edition published 2003.

Designed by Melodie Wertelet

ISBN 0-06-056966-2   ISBN 978-0-06-056966-2

12 RRD 40 39 38 37 36 35

For my friends,

whom I love

ALSO BY LUCY GREALY

As Seen on TV: Provocations

CONTENTS

Autobiography
of a Face

Pony Party

୭

MY FRIEND STEPHEN AND I USED TO DO PONY
parties together. The festivities took place on the well-
tended lawns of the vast suburban communities that had
sprung up around Diamond D Stables in the rural acres of
Rockland County. Mrs. Daniels, the owner of Diamond
D, took advantage of the opportunity and readily dis-
patched a couple of ponies for birthday parties. In the
early years Mrs. Daniels used to attend the parties with us,
something Stephen and I dreaded. She fancied herself
a sort of Mrs. Roy Rogers and dressed in embarrassing
accordance: fringed shirts, oversized belt buckles, ram-
shackle hats. I'd stand there holding a pony, cringing inwardly with mortification as if she were my own mother.
But as we got older and Stephen got his driver's license,
and as Diamond D itself slowly sank into a somewhat
surreal, muddy, and orphaned state of anarchy, we worked
the parties by ourselves, which I relished.

We were invariably late for the birthday party, a result of

loading the ponies at the last minute, combined with our truly remarkable propensity for getting lost. I never really minded, though. I enjoyed the drive through those precisely planned streets as the summer air swirled through the cab of the pickup, rustling the crepe-paper ribbons temporarily draped over the rear-view mirror. When we finally found our destination, we'd clip the ribbons into the ponies' manes and tails in a rather sad attempt to imbue a festive air. The neighborhoods were varied, from close, tree-laden streets crammed with ranch-style houses to more spacious boulevards dotted with outsized Tudors. Still, all the communities seemed to share a certain carbon-copy quality: house after house looked exactly like the one next to it, save for the occasional cement deer or sculpted shrub. A dog would always appear and chase the trailer for a set number of lawns — some mysterious canine demarcation of territory — before suddenly dropping away, to be replaced by another dog running and barking behind us a few lawns later.

I liked those dogs, liked their sense of purpose and enjoyment and responsibility. I especially liked being lost, tooling through strange neighborhoods with Stephen. As we drove by the houses, I gazed into the windows, imagining what the families inside were like. My ideas were loosely based on what I had learned from TV and films. I pictured a father in a reclining chair next to a lamp, its shade trimmed with small white tassels. Somewhere nearby a wife in a coordinated outfit chatted on the phone with friends while their children set the dinner table. As they ate their home-cooked food, passing assorted white serving dishes, they'd casually ask each other about the day. Perhaps someone would mention the unusual sight of a horse trailer going past the house that day. Certain that these families were nothing like my own, a certainty wrought with a sense of vague superiority and even vaguer longing, I took pride and pleasure in knowing that I was the person in that strangely surreal trailer with the kicking ponies and angry muffler, that I had driven by their house that day, that I had brushed against their lives, and past them, like that.

Once we reached the party, there was a great rush of excitement. The children, realizing that the ponies had arrived, would come running from the back yard in their silly hats; their now forgotten balloons, bobbing colorfully behind them, would fly off in search of some tree or telephone wire. The ponies, reacting to the excitement of new sounds and smells, would promptly take a crap in the driveway, to a chorus of disgusted groans.

My pleasure at the sight of the children didn't last long, however. I knew what was coming. As soon as they got over the thrill of being near the ponies, they'd notice me. Half my jaw was missing, which gave my face a strange triangular shape, accentuated by the fact that I was unable to keep my mouth completely closed. When I first started doing pony parties, my hair was still short and wispy, still growing in from the chemo. But as it grew I made things worse by continuously bowing my head and hiding behind the curtain of hair, furtively peering out at the world like some nervous actor. Unlike the actor, though, I didn't secretly relish my audience, and if it were possible I would have stood behind that curtain forever, my head bent in an eternal act of deference. I was, however, dependent upon my audience. Their approval or disapproval defined everything for me, and I believed with every cell in my body that approval wasn't written into my particular script. I was fourteen years old.

"I *hate* this, why am I doing this?" I'd ask myself each time, but I had no choice if I wanted to keep my job at the stable. Everyone who worked at Diamond D had to do pony parties — no exceptions. Years later a friend remarked how odd it was that an adult would even think to send a disfigured child to work at a kid's party, but at the time it was never an issue. If my presence in these back yards was something of an anomaly, it wasn't just because of my face. In fact, my physical oddness seemed somehow to fit in with the general oddness and failings of Diamond D.

The stable was a small place near the bottom of a gently sloping hill. Each spring the melting snow left behind ankle-deep mud that wouldn't dry up completely until midsummer. Mrs. Daniels possessed a number of peculiar traits that made life at Diamond D unpredictable. When she wasn't trying to save our souls, or treating Stephen's rumored homosexuality by unexpectedly exposing her breasts to him, she was taking us on shoplifting sprees, dropping criminal hints like some Artful Dodger.

No one at Diamond D knew how to properly care for horses. Most of the animals were kept outside in three small, grassless corrals. The barn was on the verge of collapse; our every entry was accompanied by the fluttering sounds of startled rats. The "staff" consisted of a bunch of junior high and high school kids willing to work in exchange for riding privileges. And the main source of income, apart from pony parties, was hacking — renting out the horses for ten dollars an hour to anyone willing to pay. Mrs. Daniels bought the horses at an auction whose main customer was the meat dealer for a dog-food company; Diamond D, more often than not, was merely a way station. The general air of neglect surrounding the stable was the result more of ignorance than of apathy. It's not as if we didn't care about the horses — we simply didn't know any better. And for most of us, especially me, Diamond D was a haven. Though I had to suffer through the pony parties, I was more willing to do so to spend time alone with the horses. I considered animals bearers of higher truth, and I wanted to align myself with their knowledge. I thought animals were the only beings capable of understanding me.

I had finished chemotherapy only a few months before I started looking in the Yellow Pages for stables where I might work. Just fourteen and still unclear about the exact details of my surgery, I made my way down the listings. It was the July Fourth weekend, and Mrs. Daniels, typically overbooked, said I had called at exactly the right moment. Overjoyed, I went into the kitchen to tell my mother I had a job at a stable. She looked at me dubiously.

"Did you tell them about yourself?"

I hesitated, and lied. "Yes, of course I did."

"Are you sure they know you were sick? Will you be up for this?"

"Of *course* I am," I replied in my most petulant adolescent tone.

In actuality it hadn't even occurred to me to mention cancer, or my face, to Mrs. Daniels. I was still blissfully unaware, somehow believing that the only reason people stared at me was because my hair was still growing in. So my mother obligingly drove all sixty-odd pounds of me down to Diamond D, where my pale and misshapen face seemed to surprise all of us. They let me water a few horses, imagining I wouldn't last more than a day. I stayed for four years.

That first day I walked a small pinto in circle after circle, practically drunk with the aroma of the horses. But with each circle, each new child lifted into the tiny saddle, I became more and more uncomfortable, and with each circuit my head dropped just a little bit further in shame. With time I became adept at handling the horses, and even more adept at avoiding the direct stares of the children.

When our trailer pulled into the driveway for a pony party, I would briefly remember my own excitement at being around ponies for the first time. But I also knew that these children lived apart from me. Through them I learned the language of paranoia: every whisper I heard was a comment about the way I looked, every laugh a joke at my expense.

Partly I was honing my self-consciousness into a torture device, sharp and efficient enough to last me the rest of my

How do I react to
deformity —
Talk abt a scar

life. Partly I was right: they *were* staring at me, laughing at me. The cruelty of children is immense, almost startling in its precision. The kids at the parties were fairly young and, surrounded by adults, they rarely made cruel remarks outright. But their open, uncensored stares were more painful than the deliberate taunts of my peers at school, where insecurities drove everything and everyone like some looming, evil presence in a haunted machine. But in those back yards, where the grass was mown so short and sharp it would have hurt to walk on it, there was only the fact of me, my face, my ugliness.

This singularity of meaning — I *was* my face, I *was* ugliness — though sometimes unbearable, also offered a possible point of escape. It became the launching pad from which to lift off, the one immediately recognizable place to point to when asked what was wrong with my life. Everything led to it, everything receded from it — my face as personal vanishing point. The pain these children brought with their stares engulfed every other pain in my life. Yet occasionally, just as that vast ocean threatened to swallow me whole, some greater force would lift me out and enable me to walk among them easily and carelessly, as alien as the pony that trotted beside me, his tail held high in excitement, his nostrils wide in anticipation of a brief encounter with a world beyond his comprehension.

The parents would trail behind the kids, iced drinks clinking, making their own, more practical comments about the fresh horse manure in their driveway. If Stephen and I liked their looks (all our judgments were instantaneous), we'd shovel it up; if not, we'd tell them cleanup wasn't included in the fee. Stephen came from a large, all-American family, but for me these grownups provided a secret fascination. The mothers had frosted lipstick and long bright fingernails; the fathers sported gold watches and smelled of too much aftershave.

This was the late seventies, and a number of corporate headquarters had sprung up across the border in New Jersey. Complete with duck ponds and fountains, these "industrial parks" looked more like fancy hotels than office buildings. The newly planted suburban lawns I found myself parading ponies on were a direct result of their proliferation.

My feelings of being an outsider were strengthened by the reminder of what my own family didn't have: money. We *should* have had money: this was true in practical terms, for my father was a successful journalist, and it was also true within my family mythology, which conjured up images of Fallen Aristocracy. We were displaced foreigners, Europeans newly arrived in an alien landscape. If we had had the money we felt entitled to, we would never have spent it on anything as mundane as a house in Spring Valley or as silly and trivial as a pony party.

Unfortunately, the mythologically endowed money didn't materialize. Despite my father's good job with a major television network, we were barraged by collection agencies, and our house was falling apart around us. Either unwilling or unable, I'm not sure which, to spend money on plumbers and electricians and general handymen, my father kept our house barely together by a complex system of odd bits of wire, duct tape, and putty, which he applied rather haphazardly and good-naturedly on weekend afternoons. He sang when he worked. Bits of opera, slapped together jauntily with the current top forty and ancient ditties from his childhood, were periodically interrupted as he patiently explained his work to the dog, who always listened attentively.

Anything my father fixed usually did not stay fixed for more than a few months. Flushing our toilets when it rained required coaxing with a Zenlike ritual of jiggles to avoid spilling the entire contents of the septic tank onto the basement floor. One walked by the oven door with a sense of near reverence, lest it fall open with an operatic crash. Pantheism ruled.

Similarly, when dealing with my mother, one always had to act in a delicate and prescribed way, though the exact rules of protocol seemed to shift frequently and without advance notice. One day, running out of milk was a problem easily dealt with, but on the next it was a symbol of her children's selfishness, our father's failure, and her tragic, wasted life. Lack of money, it was driven into us, was the root of all our unhappiness. So as Stephen and I drove through those "bourgeois" suburbs (my radical older brothers had taught me to identify them as such), I genuinely believed that if our family were as well-off as those families, the extra carton of milk would not have been an issue, and my mother would have been more than delighted to buy gallon after gallon until the house fairly spilled over with fresh milk.

Though our whole family shared the burden of my mother's anger, in my heart I suspected that part of it was my fault and my fault alone. Cancer is an obscenely expensive illness; I saw the bills, I heard their fights. There was no doubt that I was personally responsible for a great deal of my family's money problems: ergo, I was responsible for my mother's unhappy life. During my parents' many fights over money, I would sit in the kitchen in silence, unable to move even after my brothers and sisters had fled to their bedrooms. I sat listening as some kind of penance.

The parents who presided over the pony parties never fought, or at least not about anything significant, of this I felt sure. Resentment made me scorn them, their gauche houses, their spoiled children. These feelings might have been purely political, like those of my left-wing brothers (whose philosophies I understood very little of), if it weren't for the painfully personal detail of my face.

"What's wrong with her face?"

The mothers bent down to hear this question and, still bent over, they'd look over at me, their glances refracting away as quickly and predictably as light through a prism. I couldn't always hear their response, but I knew from experience that vague pleas for politeness would hardly satisfy a child's curiosity.

While the eyes of these perfectly formed children swiftly and deftly bored into the deepest part of me, the glances from their parents provided me with an exotic sense of power as I watched them inexpertly pretend not to notice me. After I passed the swing sets and looped around to pick up the next child waiting near the picnic table littered with cake plates, juice bottles, and party favors, I'd pause confrontationally, like some Dickensian ghost, imagining that my presence served as an uneasy reminder of what might be. What had happened to me was any parent's nightmare, and I allowed myself to believe that I was dangerous to them. The parents obliged me in this: they brushed past me, around me, sometimes even smiled at me. But not once in the three or so years that I worked pony parties did anyone ask me directly what had happened.

They were uncomfortable because of my face. I ignored the deep hurt by allowing the side of me that was desperate for any kind of definition to staunchly act out, if not exactly relish, this macabre status.

Zoom lenses, fancy flash systems, perfect focus — these cameras probably were worth more than the ponies instigating the pictures. A physical sense of dread came over me as soon as I spotted the thickly padded case, heard the sound of the zipper, noted the ridiculous, almost surgical protection provided by the fitted foam compartment. I'd automatically hold the pony's halter, careful to keep his head tight and high in case he suddenly decided to pull down for a bite of lawn. I'd expertly turn my own head away, pretending I was only just then aware of something more important off to the side. I'd tilt away at exactly the same angle each time, my hair falling in a perfect sheet of camouflage between me and the camera.

I stood there perfectly still, just as I had sat for countless medical photographs: full face, turn to the left, the right, now a three-quarter shot to the left. I took a certain pride in knowing the routine so well. I've even seen some of these medical photographs in publications. Curiously, those sterile, bright photos are easy for me to look at. For one thing, I know that only doctors look at them, and perhaps I'm even slightly proud that I'm such an interesting case, worthy of documentation. Or maybe I do not really think it is me sitting there, *Case 3, figure 6-A.*

Once, when my doctor left me waiting too long in his examining room, I leafed through my file, which I knew was strictly off-limits. I was thrilled to find a whole section of slides housed in a clear plastic folder. Removing one, I lifted it up to the fluorescent light, stared for a moment, then carefully, calmly replaced it. It was a photograph taken of me on the operating table. Most of the skin of the right side of my face had been pulled over and back, exposing something with the general shape of a face and neck but with the color and consistency of raw steak. A clamp gleamed off to the side, holding something unidentifiable in place. I wasn't particularly bothered; I've always had a fascination with gore, and had it been someone else I'd have stared endlessly. But I simply put the slide in its slot and made a mental note not to look at slides from my file again, ever.

With the same numbed yet cavalier stance, I waited for a father to click the shutter. At least these were photographs I'd never have to see, though to this day I fantasize about meeting someone who eventually shows me their photo album and there, inexplicably, in the middle of a page, is me holding a pony. I have seen one pony party photo of me. In it I'm holding on to a small dark bay pony whose name I don't remember. I look frail and thin and certainly peculiar, but I don't look anywhere near as repulsive as I then believed I did. There's a gaggle of children around me, waiting for their turn on the pony. My stomach was always in knots then, surrounded by so many children, but I can tell by my expression that I'm convincing myself I don't care as I point to the back of the line. The children look older than most of the kids at the backyard parties: some of them are even older than nine, the age I was when I got sick. I'm probably thinking about this, too, as I order them into line.

I can still hear the rubbery, metallic thud of hooves on the trailer's ramp as we loaded the ponies back into the hot and smelly box for the ride back to Diamond D. Fifteen years later, when I see that photo, I am filled with questions I rarely allow myself, such as, how do we go about turning into the people we are meant to be? What relation do the human beings in that picture have to the people they are now? How is it that all of us were caught together in that brief moment of time, me standing there pretending I wasn't hurt by a single thing in this world while they lined up for their turn on the pony, some of them excited and some of them scared, but all of them neatly, at my insistence, one in front of the other, like all the days ahead.

ONE

Luck

∽

KER-POW!

I was knocked into the present, the unmistakable *now*, by Joni Friedman's head as it collided with the right side of my jaw. Up until that moment my body had been running around within the confines of a circle of fourth-grade children gathered for a game of dodge ball, but my mind had been elsewhere. For the most part I was an abysmal athlete, and I was deeply embarrassed whenever I failed to jump bravely and deftly into a whirring jumprope, ever threatening to sting if I miscrossed its invisible boundaries, like some science-fiction force field. Or worse, when I was the weak link yet again in the school relay race. How could one doubt that the order in which one was picked for the softball team was anything but concurrent with the order in which Life would be handing out favors?

Not that I considered myself a weak or easily frightened person; in more casual games I excelled, especially at wrestling (I could beat every boy but one on my street), playing war (a known sneak, I was always called upon to be the scout), and in taking dares (I would do just about anything, no matter how ludicrous or dangerous, though I drew the line at eating invertebrates and amphibians). I was accorded a certain amount of respect in my neighborhood, not only because I once jumped out of a second-story window, but also because I would kiss an old and particularly smelly neighborhood dog on the lips whenever asked. I was a tomboy par excellence.

But when games turned official under the auspices of the Fleetwood Elementary Phys-Ed Department, everything changed. The minute a whistle appeared and boundaries were called, I transformed into *a spaz*. It all seemed so unfair: I *knew* in my heart I had great potential, star potential even, but my knowing didn't translate into hitting the ball that was coming my way. I resigned myself early on, even though I knew I could outread, outspell, and outtest the strongest kid in the classroom. And when I was picked practically last for crazy kickball or crab relays, I defeatedly assumed a certain lackadaisical attitude, which partially accounts for my inattention on the day my jaw collided with Joni Friedman's head.

Maybe I was wondering whether Colleen's superiority at dodge ball would be compromised by her all-consuming crush on David Cassidy, or maybe some other social dilemma of prepubescence ruled that day's game. I do know that the ball I was going for was *mine*. I hadn't even bothered to call it, it was so obvious, and though it was also obvious that Joni was going to try to steal it away from me, I stood my ground. The whistle to stop playing began to blow just as the ball came toward us, toward me. I leaned forward and Joni lunged sideways, and suddenly all thoughts about Colleen's social status or Joni's ethics were suddenly and sharply knocked out of me.

I felt the force of our collision in every one of my atoms as I sat, calm and lucid though slightly dazed, on the asphalt. Everyone was running to get on line. I assume Joni asked me how I was, but all I remember is sitting there among the blurred and running legs, rubbing the right side of my jaw, fascinated by how much pain I was in and by how strangely peaceful I felt. It wasn't the sensation of things happening in slow motion, which I had experienced during other minor accidents; it was as if time had mysteriously but logically shifted onto another plane. I felt as if I could speculate and theorize about a thousand different beautiful truths all in the time it would take my lips to form a single word. In retrospect, I think it's possible I had a concussion.

My jaw throbbed. Rubbing it with my hand seemed to have no good or bad effect: the pain was deep and untouchable. Because the pain was genuinely unanticipated, there was no residue of anxiety to alter my experience of it. Anxiety and anticipation, I was to learn, are the essential ingredients in *suffering* from pain, as opposed to feeling pain pure and simple. This alien ache was probably my first and last experience of unadulterated pain, which perplexed me more than it hurt me.

"Are you all right, dear?"

Interrupted in my twilight, I looked up to see Mrs. Minkin, who was on playground duty that afternoon. She fell into the category of "scary" adults, and from there into the subcategory of adults "with cooties." In her plaid wool skirts and thick makeup, luridly ugly to schoolchildren's eyes, Mrs. Minkin was not someone to whom I was willing to admit distress.

"I'm fine, thank you."

And I was fine: as quickly as it had happened, the sharp ache in my jaw receded and my sense of self transported itself back to the playground. I quickly stood up and brushed myself off. The looming issue now was how far back in line I would have to stand because of this bothersome delay. By the time I was back in the classroom I had forgotten the incident entirely.

I was reminded of it again that evening as I sat on the living room rug earnestly trying to whip up a book report I had been putting off for two weeks. Now, to my grave dismay, the report was due the very next day. Gradually I became aware of possible salvation: I had a toothache. This wasn't as welcome a reason for staying home from school as a cold or a fever because it would entail a visit to the dentist. Had it been only a minor toothache I'd probably have preferred to suffer the wrath of my teacher rather than my mother's inevitable agitation, but now that I had noticed the ache it seemed to be worsening steadily.

The dentist and I were already well acquainted. I was cursed with terrible teeth. We were told it was a common trait among people of Anglo-Irish descent, but my mother felt personally affronted by this bit of information and, as if by osmosis, I too felt a sense of shame about my teeth.

Dr. Singer convinced my parents that if there was to be any chance of my having normal adult teeth growing in, he must be allowed, posthaste, to do everything imaginable to my baby teeth. I can't even remember the work he did, but it seemed as if I went to the dentist every week for some mysterious procedure. No one likes the dentist, but what I resented most about Dr. Singer was that he made a practice of lying to me.

"Hold out your thumb and I'll show you how I'll make your tooth go to sleep so that nothing will hurt it."

I'd hold my thumb out.

"You see, I'll put this medicine on your tooth just like I'm putting it on your thumb," he'd say as he pushed a syringe lightly into my finger, releasing a jet of clear fluid.

"It won't hurt any more than that."

Then he'd turn to his instrument tray, his back blocking my view, and switch syringes. Before I could see what flashed before me, he'd stick the needle deftly into my waiting gums. I was always surprised that a simple stream of fluid could hurt so much. Even after he had performed this dirty trick many times, I believed there must be something extraordinarily wrong with my gums. I suspected I had some terrible problem in my mouth and, afraid that complaining would only bring some new and certainly painful treatment, I kept my suspicions to myself.

As the evening wore on, I could no longer pretend the toothache wasn't there. Finally I went to my mother and confessed my pain in the guarded tone I might use to admit the loss or destruction of something valuable. As I had expected, she was angry. Of course, she was angry at the situation, at the bother, at the possible cost, but at that age I had no way to distinguish such subtle gradations. I painfully presumed that her anger was directed at me alone.

Only when my father walked into the room and asked what was going on did I remember my collision earlier in the day. This new information seemed to irritate my mother even more, especially when my father, characteristically trying to dissolve the tension of the situation, ventured the prognosis "She's just got a cold in her tooth, that's all. She'll be fine in the morning."

He meant well, but his dismissal of the problem confirmed my mother's belief that she was the only one in the family who faced facts. This was true in a sense, but she never recognized that her anger scared all of us into retreat. By churning problems through her own personal mill, she kept us from ever discussing a problem outright, which, in turn, exacerbated the problem. My mother was always particularly annoyed when my father put on his good-fellow-Irishman act and dispensed comforting misinformation about the world, such as the backward notion that a tooth could have a cold in it. I was sent off to bed with two aspirins and a promise of reappraisal.

"You've got lockjaw!"

My brothers pronounced this happily the next morning, obviously excited by the idea.

I mumbled back to them as best I could.

They were only too pleased to describe in detail how I would never open my mouth again, that everything I ate from now on would have to come through a straw. It was true that I had woken up with my jaw swollen and seemingly locked — it didn't hurt when I tried to open it so much as it appeared to be stuck — but a diet of milkshakes didn't seem like such an awful fate. Primarily, however, I was excited by the idea that something really *was* wrong with me, that I hadn't been overacting the previous night, as I had allowed myself to believe; I was authentically sick — no school *definitely.* I felt cheerful. My mother made an appointment for me to see the family doctor later that morning.

"Well, considering the swelling and this immobility and that she had a hard knock, I'd say it's probably fractured."

A broken jaw. This would be the first of many diagnoses and surely the one most completely off course. Dr. Cantor explained plainly to me that if it was broken I'd have to have it wired shut so it could heal, but first I had to go over to the hospital to have it x-rayed. I wasn't particularly thrilled with the wired-shut part, but I was too involved with the idea of venturing off to a hospital emergency room to think much about it. My two absolute, hands-down favorite television programs were *Emergency!* and *Medical Center,* and the possibility of personally living out one of these thirty-minute dramas elated me. My mother kindly indulged me as I sat on a trolley in one of the curtained cubicles, humoring me about what an adventure it all was and how jealous my brothers would be that I was the principal player in such a drama. She told me how brave I was and how lucky we all were that this had happened to me and not Sarah, my twin sister, an avowed scaredy-cat. Sarah would have cried horrendously, but I was courageous and didn't cry and thus was good. It seemed a natural enough equation at the time.

The x-rays came back: it wasn't a broken jaw, but something called a dental cyst, probably caused by the blow to my jaw forcing one of my back molars down into the gum, nicking the mandible. It was nothing serious, but they would have to operate and remove the cyst right away to avoid an infection. I went back home with my mother to collect my pajamas, and off we went to Pascack Valley Hospital, a small community hospital in the next town over. Surgery was scheduled for the following day.

What I remember most from that first night in the hospital is that I didn't sleep very much. I devoted most of the time to a silly conversation about David Cassidy with the girl in the bed across from me. Also I had to have my temperature taken throughout the night to monitor possible infection, and much to the delight of my neighbor, who stood up in her bed to watch, my nurse insisted on taking it rectally without bothering to draw the curtain. My neighbor giggled and I thought her a fool, but I didn't yet have enough resources of dignity to do anything except giggle along with her at my absurd situation. At midnight a nurse came along and taped an NPO sign to my bed: Nil Per Oral, nothing by mouth. I felt special, singled out, and I allowed myself a condescending tone as I explained to my neighbor what it meant, just as the nurse had explained it to me thirty seconds before.

*　　*　　*

Every hospital has its own quirky protocol. Some hospitals make you put on the surgical gown in your room, some make you wait until you reach the O.R. Some anesthesia departments have rooms in which you are put to sleep, others take you right on into the operating room itself. Pascack Valley Hospital subscribed to the latter and also, bless their hearts, to the theory that it's best to knock the patient out as quickly as possible and *then* assign the IV's and other assorted needles and tubes to their final bodily destinations. Medically this isn't the most desirable procedure, as there should be instant access to the blood and airway systems in case anything goes suddenly awry during the initial stages of administering gas. Presumably this small pediatrics department figured it wasn't worth all the tears, screams, and struggling: get the conscious entity out of the way as quickly as possible, then insert instruments to your heart's content.

Still living in the fantasy of a television show, and slightly dopey both from the pre-op medication and from my sleepless night, I was impressed with the sight of a real live operating room, just as I had been pleased by my view of the corridor ceiling during the trolley ride down there. I was somewhat disappointed when I failed to detect a glass-domed amphitheater through which row after row of doctors would peer down, intrigued by my fascinating case, but the gleaming metal and impressive lights, exactly as I'd anticipated, placated me. My first authentic surgically masked face peered down at me, blocking the bright light from the overhead lamp.

"I'm going to put this mask over your face and give

you some air to make you sleepy, it might smell a little funny."

Funny was an understatement. Through the black rubber mask came chemical fumes, so alien to me that I could never have imagined such a smell existed. I thought I would suffocate. I struggled slightly, trying to turn my head away and reach for the mask with my hands. Someone I couldn't see reached out and grasped my hands, squeezing them too tightly, while someone else put his hand on my forehead. This last gesture calmed me instantly.

"Now I want you to close your eyes and breathe and relax and think about some nice things. Do you have any pets?"

I began to list the names of the menagerie back home, aware that a faint buzzing was growing louder and louder. The things around me began to lose their borders. The doctor's face and the bodies of people hovering nearby no longer appeared in terms of what they were but in terms of what they were not. It became increasingly difficult to speak. After listing the names of two cats, I was reduced to producing only a syllable at a time with each breath, and even that seemed like a great effort.

"Close your eyes."

This was unthinkable. First, I didn't want to miss a thing, and second, what if they thought I was asleep and began cutting me open when I was merely resting my eyes? This last fear was to haunt me through subsequent operations. Even after I admitted my fear a couple of years later and had the whole process patiently explained, I remained wary.

I felt nauseated. The gas was overpowering, the buzz now drowning everything else out, and finally I couldn't take it any longer and rolled over to vomit. A viscous magenta liquid with swirls of green poured out and created an interesting stain on the white sheet. I must have groaned, because someone put a metal basin near me, into which I vainly tried to deposit more of the smelly but curiously pleasant concoction. I still felt nauseous but could bring nothing else up. I lay back and closed my eyes, exhausted from the effort. A strange nurse was standing beside my bed insisting I acknowledge her visually and then, to my great annoyance, verbally. The very last thing I wanted to do just then was open my eyes, let alone speak to this woman, who was now asking the most ridiculous question I'd ever heard: Lucinda, what time is it? I wasn't used to people calling me by my full given name. With an outstretched arm she directed my gaze to a clock on the wall. This is nonsense, I thought. Couldn't she understand that sleeping was the single most desirable act in the world, the only thing I could ever want to do with the rest of my life? She asked me a third time, and only to rid myself of her I gathered my wits and focusing powers and told her. It was eleven-ten. My first operation was over.

Six months later, sometime near Easter, I came home from school with the right side of my face swollen and hot. I'd been going in to the hospital sporadically to have x-rays taken of my jaw ever since the first surgery. A bony knob had appeared on the very tip of my jaw just under my ear shortly after the initial surgery, and my mother had asked the doctor about it repeatedly.

"It's just a bony growth; it's nothing to worry about, Mrs. Grealy."

"But surely it's not normal, a young girl to have a lump like that on her face?"

"It's just a bony growth, Mrs. Grealy, nothing unusual after such surgery."

The doctor, who wasn't a doctor but a specialized dentist, smiled condescendingly after each inquiry. Nothing infuriated my mother more than this condescension, which even I recognized as endemic in the medical profession. Unfortunately for my mother, I was still a typical nine-year-old, and I seized upon every opportunity to be embarrassed by her. Why did she have to make such a fuss? Couldn't she just accept what they said? Not brave enough to actually speak up, I mentally rolled my eyes at each encounter between my mother and the doctor.

If I had suspected how classic and common my tendency toward parental shame was I'd surely have abandoned it and sided with my mother. I was vain and proud when it came to wanting to be different from everyone else. I wanted nothing more than to be special, and so far the role of patient had delivered. My teachers had given me a noticeable amount of special treatment, and I'd gained a new level of respect from my friends since going under the knife.

When my mother marched me back to Dr. Cantor's office, it was with a sense almost of righteousness. It was obvious I had a bad infection that they could no longer ignore, and my heart thrilled when I heard the words "emergency surgery" used in conjunction with my name. They had to drain and clean out the lump, which was growing almost visibly and looking angrier by the minute. I asked if I'd get to go to the hospital in an ambulance and was abjectly disappointed when told no.

As far as I was concerned, I was still on a great adventure, the star of my own television special. Up until that point my great trials in life had been the emotional upheavals of our painful family situation. This physical drama seemed a bit of light relief to me. Besides, there was yet another unfinished book report looming. Just when I thought it was hopeless, I'd again been handed this brilliant stroke of luck. Something as impressive-sounding as Emergency Surgery had to be worth as long an extension as I could ask for, as well as another round of presents. It seems odd to me now that a deed as relatively easy as not crying over a needle was rewarded so lavishly, while my Herculean efforts to simply not fall apart during one of the many family crises went completely unnoticed.

After the surgery my parents were instructed to take me to the Strang Clinic, which translated to me as a trip to the City. I was thrilled: I loved any chance to drive through the filthy, bewildering streets of New York, see so many different types of people, marvel that so many noises could exist all at once — horns, sirens, human yells. At the Strang we met the eccentric Dr. John Conley, a leader in the field of head and neck surgery. After a thorough examination, he arranged to have me admitted to the children's wing of Columbia Presbyterian Hospital, known as Babies Hospital.

When a film's heroine innocently coughs, you know that two scenes later, at most, she'll be in an oxygen tent; when a man bumps into a woman at the train station, you know that man will become the woman's lover and/or murderer. In everyday life, where we cough often and are always bumping into people, our daily actions rarely reverberate so lucidly. Once we love or hate someone, we can think back and remember that first casual encounter. But what of all the chance meetings that nothing ever comes of? While our bodies move ever forward on the time line, our minds continuously trace backward, seeking shape and meaning as deftly as any arrow seeking its mark.

As I sat there on the playground's sticky asphalt I experienced time in a new way, but perhaps that memory has significance because of the way my life has unfolded. It seems almost uncanny to me that I didn't know; how could I not have? A year before, my class had gone on a field trip to a museum where I became fascinated with a medieval chart showing how women contained minute individuals, all perfectly formed and lined up like so many sardines in a can, just below their navels. What's more, these individuals contained more minute versions of themselves, who in turn held even more. Our fates were already perfectly mapped out within us, just as we once waited perfectly inside of our mothers, who themselves were held within the depths of their mothers, our great-grandmothers.

It's impossible for me not to revisit this twenty-year-old playground scene and wonder why I didn't go right when I should have gone left, or, alternatively, see my movements as inexorable. If the cancer was already there, it would have been discovered eventually, though probably too late.

Or perhaps that knock set in motion a chain of physical events that created an opportunity for the cancer to grow which it might not otherwise have found. Sometimes it is as difficult to know what the past holds as it is to know the future, and just as an answer to a riddle seems so obvious once it is revealed, it seems curious to me now that I passed through all those early moments with no idea of their weight.

Petting Zoo

AT FIRST THERE WAS ONLY THE PRESENCE OF THE boy beneath the bed to horrify me, but before I knew it his father was under there, and then, most shocking of all, even the doctor squatted down and tried his own ineffectual cajoling. This last bit of vaudeville was too much; not only were the doctor's assurances on par with some villain's comforting homilies, but it was all so . . . so . . . *undignified.* I was mortified. The boy, a year or two younger than me, wore red pajamas with feet; his father was almost completely bald and wore thick glasses. He reminded me of a father-actor on a black and white TV show I watched in reruns every afternoon after school. Partly I felt embarrassed for the father and the doctor, though I also maintained a degree of scorn toward them for indulging the boy's behavior. But mostly I found myself deeply embarrassed for the boy. How could anyone sink so low as to hide beneath a bed? This went against every belief I held dear. One had to be good. One must never complain or struggle. One must never, under any circumstances, show fear and, prime directive above all, one must never, ever cry. I was nothing if not harsh. Had I not found myself in this role of sick child, I would have made an equally good fascist or religious martyr. The subtleties of my first visit to the emergency room, where I'd been praised as good for being brave, were already arranging themselves into a personal treatise in much the same way that a seemingly inconsequential architectural miscalculation on the ground floor can result in a sweeping chasm in the penthouse. At a time when everything in my family was unpredictable and dysfunctional, with my mother recently discharged from a brief stay in a hospital herself, here I had been supplied with a formula of behavior for gaining acceptance and, I believed, love. All I had to do was perform heroically and I could personally save my entire family.

At that point heroism was still fairly easy: I'd been on Ward 10 in Babies Hospital for only about an hour. I wasn't happy about being associated with babies, but I was thrilled by the notion of being in the city, in a hospital that had twelve floors and an elevator. To this day I find riding in an elevator a basically pleasing act, the progression of lights marking a sense of excited anticipation. Ward 10 was an old ward. Babies Hospital was nothing like the shining, clean techno-miracles I was used to on television and had experienced at the considerably newer Pascack Valley Hospital. The walls were pale green, and the floor was dark green tiles speckled with gray, worn to an even darker shade where people had paced over the years. All the doors were wood, and the partitions, strategically placed for viewing purposes, were made of thick sea-green glass reinforced with mesh wire. There were bars on all of the outside windows. Though the hospital was undeniably clean, a dingy air prevailed throughout. I was always a fan of the gleaming new, but in time I came to find this dinginess comforting, more humane than the fascinating but alien landscapes of newer wards I would later visit.

I heard my name called. Again they called me Lucinda. Previously that name had belonged only to the first day of school, but from that moment on I recognized it as the property of all people in uniforms standing in the unflattering fluorescent light of hospitals. The doctor asked my parents a number of questions about my mother's pregnancy and my infancy, and sometimes my mother and father had to confer with each other in order to answer. I wasn't used to seeing my parents defer to people in positions of authority; I wasn't used to seeing them act together, pair up like this; and I wasn't used to seeing them act so *normal,* like the parents of the friends in my neighborhood, like parents I had seen on TV. It was generally assumed that we were not a normal family, a feeling we proudly carried and tried to hide at the same time.

We — my parents, two older brothers, older sister, twin sister, and I — had immigrated to America five years earlier, when Sarah and I were four. My father, a well-known television journalist in Ireland, had been offered a job he couldn't refuse with a major network in the States. He packed us all up and, in what was probably meant to be some sort of tongue-in-cheek joke about immigrants, had us travel to America by boat. Unlike our earlier country-men, who came in steerage, we sailed on the *Queen Mary*, on what was her penultimate voyage. Surely this grand act was to be the harbinger of the riches already awaiting us. As with most of my father's gestures, that voyage was well meant, but later, when things were not going quite as well, it was referred to with scorn, and even later, after his early death, it seemed an act filled with literary bathos, and pointedly sad.

Of course, at the time it was an adventure extraordi-naire, especially for a four-year-old gathering first memo-ries. My brothers used to play Ping-Pong on a back deck and sometimes lost the ball over the side. I loved nothing better than to run and stare at its lostness in the churning water far below. The chaos held me tightly, endlessly. One day Sarah drank a glass of cream instead of milk and was sick all over the place; another time we were invited to a children's party in the gigantic ballroom, and I won a prize at Duck Duck Goose. In the ship's gym there was an electric horse and a peculiar machine with a large strap that vigorously jiggled the fat atoms in your bottom to smithereens. The most predictable memory of all, the Statue of Liberty, draws a complete blank, but I remember looking up and simultaneously hoping and fearing that the ship's stack would hit the Verrazano Bridge as we passed beneath it. New York, when we disembarked, was rainy and filled with broken windows.

"Where are we now?" Sarah and I asked our mother several days later in our new kitchen. She stood near the sink, her hair short and ash blond, her shirt white silk. I was convinced my mother was the most beautiful woman in the world.

"We're in Spring Valley now." She was patient with us.

"But when are we going to America?"

This struck her as funny. Her face lit up and I knew we'd pleased her, but exactly how escaped me. Spring Valley was just a name, a place, but America, now that was something big, a whole way of life, an idea, a piece of magic. Judging by the way everyone spoke of it all the time, I was eager to know when we were going to be there.

My oldest brother, Sean, was seventeen when we left Dublin, Nicholas a few years younger than he, and Suellen a few years younger than that. For Sarah and me, Dublin was just a collection of vague shadows, but for the rest of our siblings, Ireland was home. This new place to which they'd been unwillingly transported, America, could never match up. The virtues of Ireland and England were constantly extolled. Many years later, when I moved away from the country I'd grown up in, I came to understand how small things from that previous life such as a brand of candy or a particular television show took on great symbolic meaning.

But these transformations of loss and symbol came much later. When we first arrived, I could not even eat an American candy bar without being reminded by one of my brothers that it stood for the entire political and social inferiority of America. Sometimes a Crunchie, a British/Irish candy bar, would appear in the house — perhaps someone had mailed it — and the feel of that orange wrapper in my hand seemed to conjure everything that

I was missing. Television, I was reminded, was vastly superior back in Ireland. I watched American shows and felt guilty for liking them, wondered why their counterparts across the ocean were so much more refined. I never doubted Ireland's superiority, I only assumed it was some failing of mine that prevented me from seeing it in precise terms.

My poor brothers, missing their home more than they could admit, felt nothing but contempt for this new country thrust upon them. Their worst insults became *That's so American; don't be so American; how American.* If we were selfish or acted spoiled, we were *becoming American.* When we used up all the hot water in the bath, that was an American thing to do. Gradually my earliest memories of Ireland transformed into pure myth. Where I was now was not only no good, it was getting worse all the time. The flawless times of the family were past; I had missed them simply by being born too late. I began a lifelong affair with nostalgia, with only the vaguest notions of what I was nostalgic for.

Apart from its vulgar culture, the worst aspect of America was its politics, according to my brothers. They had leaned toward the left back in Ireland, and in reaction to our conventional Republican neighborhood in a country different in almost every way from the one they knew, they became radical. Added to the list of insults along with *American* were *Bourgeois* and *Capitalist; American-Bourgeois-Capitalist* was the most searing of all. I had no true idea of what these things meant, but I developed a healthy disdain for them too. I remember my teacher in the third grade talking about some great and famous capitalist. It was during the first snow of the winter, and she had a hard time keeping everyone from looking out the window except for me. I sat there tensely, wondering why she was describing this man with such admiration in her voice. I was waiting to hear the awful truth of what this capitalist had done, but instead the teacher gave up and placated the class by having us make snowflakes from colored paper.

If I intuited that our family was different and in some ways superior, there were also obvious oddities about us not as easily defensible. Neighbors and schoolmates made fun of our different accents. Though I didn't understand this at the time, Sean was in the early stages of what would be diagnosed as schizophrenia. Apart from that, he had long hair and lived a "hippie" life, much different from the lives of our neighbors' sons. My mother herself suffered from depression, an illness I could not understand at the time. There were always money problems, even before my father lost his job, and if nothing else, our home's drastic state of disrepair served as a reminder that there were things I had to keep from other people.

Seeing my parents act so much like, well, *parents,* other people's parents, there on Babies 10, surprised me, and momentarily fooled me. They spent the entire afternoon with me, talking to doctors, talking to me, to each other. I met some of the other children and their parents. I watched the drama of the boy in the red-footed pajamas unfold as he was eventually extricated from beneath the bed, saw how his mother held him in her lap the entire time the doctor did whatever he was doing to him. At one

point I was sent down to Hematology for a blood test. I'd
had several blood samples taken from my arm, but this was
a finger stick. I watched the entire procedure, fascinated.
When I stood up I couldn't understand why I heard a faint
buzz and felt so lightheaded. Afterward I reported my
dizziness to my mother, who simply remarked that I had
been silly to watch. I was perplexed because I'd actually
enjoyed watching the blood test and only now felt embarrassed by my "weakling" response. Since then I've always
turned my head whenever someone approaches me with a
needle.

I visited Radiology for a chest x-ray. This department
was newly renovated and, unlike the rest of the hospital,
was painted in bright colors. It was the only floor that
actually fit my picture of a children's hospital. Murals of
cartoonish animals and clowns stared merrily at me as I
walked down the halls. In the waiting room I found an
absurd number of half-broken toys and giant stuffed animals sitting dejectedly in the corners, too big and un-
wieldy to really play with. Being all of nine years old, I
disassociated myself from all this baby stuff anyway, and
made a point of looking disdainful and bored. I'd consciously packed no stuffed animals to bring to the hospital. It was of paramount importance that I appear adult,
strong, unafraid.

As the day wore on, I began to believe that maybe my
parents really were like the other parents after all, people I
normally would have castigated for their indulgence, for
letting their worries and fears hang like pictures on a wall
for everyone to see. Finally, as dinnertime approached, the

intern who'd examined me earlier explained to my parents (I listened in as he talked about me in the third person) that he was going to do a bone marrow test on me. We were all standing in the hall together. I don't remember whether I was afraid of this test I'd never heard of, but when my parents said, "Well then, we'll be off," I looked at them panic-stricken and asked, "Aren't you going to stay with me?" They looked at each other, then back at me, and said something about the traffic, and besides, I wasn't scared, was I?

I felt my face flush. Things seemed to rush at me as if I were the focal point of some unseeable camera's close-up. Immediately I regretted all my assumptions. The embarrassment I felt then stays with me still, though of course it wasn't embarrassment. That feeling was about as different from embarrassment as a patch of soil is from a tree, an egg case from a spider, a lump of stone from a sculpted hand lying heavily on an even stonier lap. It was the moment when I understood unequivocally: I was in this alone.

As it turned out, there really wasn't much to fear, at least not just then. The treatment room was small and overheated, even cozy, being too old for fluorescent lighting. The two interns who did the bone marrow test had only arrived on the ward that day, the first of their rotation. I lay on my stomach on the stiff, clean-smelling white sheets covering the table. Outside, night was settling, but the sky was still velvety blue from the city lights. The interns seemed to know each other from working together in the past, seemed bent on entertaining each other more than me, but I liked them instantly. I had no idea who this Mutt and Jeff team was, but they had a little routine down, switching into alternately squeaky and rough voices. They even thought it was funny when they pressed down on my numbed lower spine and my legs reflexively kicked the contents of the tray all over the floor. As it clattered on the green tile I tensed, waiting for the flare of anger I normally associated with even the most innocent of accidents. Instead they laughed at themselves, made jokes silly enough that we all groaned, awarded me ludicrously high points for being such a good sport, allowed me to feel at ease, at home even.

This sense of comfort continued in the following days and weeks. There were definite problems to face here, but to me they seemed entirely manageable: lie still when you're told, be brave. It didn't seem like so much to ask, really, considering what I got in return: attention, absence from school, occasional presents, and, though I wouldn't have admitted it to anyone even if I could have articulated it, freedom from the tensions at home. My father would stop by after work to say hello when he wasn't working too late, while my mother, who hated driving into the city, came in less frequently. Some of the other visiting parents, the ones who came in every day, felt sorry for my lack of visitors and sneaked me contraband food items. I played up to this expertly whenever I sensed a particularly orphan-sensitive audience. My mother would have been appalled if she'd known. I slipped in and out of my various personae with great ease, even flair. Being a child, my past was not yet a burden to me. It was merely there, and I felt a certain freedom to suit the present to my needs, doing whatever might get me an inch somewhere.

I felt perfectly fine. Each day one test would be scheduled, typically an intricate scan or x-ray, and these were relatively painless. I made friends with the other children, quickly discovering the hierarchy on that and all other wards. The truly sick were at the top, but of course being too sick worked against you as you couldn't enjoy the status. Anyone having an operation also ranked, though we always factored in how long your operation would take, how many you'd had before, and how gruesome the resultant scar would be. But the true deciding factor was seniority, how long you'd been on the ward, and in this, Derek was king.

Derek was a handsome boy with a serious case of asthma, and, I would find out much later, he was from an unstable home, which inclined doctors to keep him in the hospital, with its warmth and wealth of food, albeit bad, longer than was medically necessary. He had been in and out of the hospital many times already, and by the time I arrived he had a week's stay under his belt. Despite his asthma he seemed to feel fine, and the two of us together, relatively healthy and with far too much time on our hands, spelled trouble.

Afternoons were long. Sunlight pushed in past the barred windows and lay down heavily on the green floor like an algae-infested lake. When the nurses shut off the bright overhead lights you could almost hear them sigh, and this was the moment Derek and I waited for each day, naptime, when the ward was quiet and the nurses sat around their station, pretending not to care what we were up to as long as we didn't make noise.

Sometimes the afternoons were planned for us. We were taken to another floor with a playroom that boasted a large, ornate dollhouse, a real collector's item probably, donated by some well-meaning person. You could only look at it from behind a glass partition, but it was too nice to be played with anyway. It was really a doll's mansion, with dozens of intricate rooms filled with luxuries like tapestries and fluffy feather comforters on brass beds. There were perfect little spoons and forks, neatly made beds with teddy bears in the children's room, a bowl of milk in the pantry with *Kitty* stenciled on it. There were also old-fashioned items, possibly of a sort still in use when the house was donated: washboards and iceboxes and chamber pots. This house had absolutely nothing to do with any of our lives. Most of the children in the hospital came from the surrounding poor neighborhood, and this little house was a rarefied version of everything they would never have and, with its protective glass partition, were not allowed to touch even in miniature. Sometimes you'd see a child standing there, staring, but for the most part the giant miniature house, despite its prominent position near the door, was ignored.

Every once in a while they showed a movie, usually just cartoons, in a lecture hall in another part of the hospital. Getting there was half the fun, passing through the main halls in our slippers and bathrobes, passing people in their street clothes. It was as if clothes spoke to each other, our childish pajamas murmuring something special about us as we brushed past the suits and white coats and work clothes. The movie itself was usually awful, but Derek and I enjoyed making fun of it later and guessing what was wrong with the other kids who filed in with us, pushing their IV poles, holding parts of themselves delicately. Anyone who looked truly shocking or particularly ill or sported an impressive piece of machinery was treated with respect. There was an implicit honor code: you never stared openly, you always did whatever you had to to help, you were always extraordinarily patient. Not that we weren't perfectly capable of being right little assholes, and indeed were in other settings, but in the hospital a kind of dignity reigned.

It was when nothing official was scheduled that Derek and I got up to our own tricks. At first we stayed on the ward, sneaking around in the storage room or any other place that carried a forbidden air. Gradually we took to sneaking off the ward, where we risked getting caught by a dutiful nurse. The lobby was attractive for its gift shop. We stole get well cards and gave them to other patients, signing them *Love and Kisses, Michael Jackson*. We thought this was hysterical. A few times we ventured down near Emergency. That waiting room had all the good magazines, and there we lived in eternal hope that someone covered in blood would stagger in through the door, maybe even clutching a knife sticking out of his heart. It never happened. Over in Postnatal we could see the minuscule preemies. They hardly looked human, caged in their incubators like rare specimens on display, hooked up to all kinds of fascinating tubes and machines. It was a good thing they'd never remember any of it, we decided, and thought this lack of memory gave us leave to ogle them in the painful technological aftermath of their precarious entrance into this world.

Though it seemed like an eternity, that hospital stay probably lasted only two weeks or so. Every day I'd have some test, and it never occurred to me to ask what was going on, what the tests were for, what the results were. At least this is how I remember it, though my mother tells it differently. In my version, when the day came, the doctors took both my parents into my room alone. They stayed in there a long time. Finally my mother emerged, explaining that I was going to have an operation on my jaw, but that I could come home for the weekend first.

I remember being thrilled, as if I'd only heard the part about going home for a weekend. My mother looked at me aghast. She was acting strangely, I thought, not herself. I had to explain that it wasn't the operation I was excited about. I knew that if I went home for a weekend I'd get special treatment, and I did. My father let me go horseback riding not once, a big treat in itself, but twice. When my sister complained about the favoritism, my father virtually snapped, an uncharacteristic response, but I was too excited by the proximity of horses, with their sweet, grimy smell, to even try to figure it out. I don't remember going to visit my school at all.

In my mother's version, when she came out of my hospital room I jumped up, hearing only that I was going home. But after that, she says, the doctor asked to speak to me, as if I were an adult. He told me I had a malignancy.

He explained they would do everything they could, that I should do my best to get well and they would help. As my mother tells it, I did go to school, where I thanked my teachers and classmates for the cards they'd sent me. I told them I had a malignancy. My mother said I seemed rather happy about it, and my teachers were shocked by my attitude. I told my teacher and all of my friends, probably with pride: I had a malignancy, I was going to have a *big* operation now.

Some years later, I don't remember exactly how many, as my family was milling about the kitchen and I was leafing through the paper at the table, someone dated an event as something that had happened "before Lucy had cancer." Shocked, I looked up.

"I had cancer?"

"Of course you did, fool, what did you think you had?"

"I thought I had a Ewing's sarcoma."

"And what on earth do you think that is?"

My family seemed rather incredulous, but it was true. In all that time, not one person ever said the word *cancer* to me, at least not in a way that registered as pertaining to me.

It was as if the earth were without form until those words were uttered, until those sounds took on decisions, themes, motifs. There may have been thousands, millions of words uttered before those incisive words, but they had no meaning, no leftover telltale shapes to show that they had existed. I loved words, the sound of them. One of my favorite experiments was to pick a word and repeat it ceaselessly to myself until I was in awe of it, until it transformed itself entirely into an absurd sound having nothing at all to do with the thing it signified. *Gull. Truck. Banana. Formula.* And then, *malignancy.* I can reconstruct now that its important syllables probably charmed me, its promise of rare and dangerous implications made me feel important, but its lack of meaning provided me with just enough echo to act as background to my shock at hearing the word *cancer.*

Lack of meaning had its own shape; it groped in the darkness, spoke to me only from a hole in the wall late at night, when I dreamed of witches who apologized profusely before inserting their singing knives into me, explaining that they were sorry, they didn't want to kill me but they had to, they were witches, it was their job. I never recognized these dreams as related to what was happening to me. I thought only of what was right in front of me, like my experiments with words, shredding their meaning through repetition. My experiments seemed no more significant than my attempts to observe the moment when I fell asleep at night, watching in the dark like some prowler for that thin line between conscious and unconscious.

I remember all the things I did with Derek very clearly and even nostalgically — going to the movies, peering through the glass at that dated dollhouse, blowing up surgical gloves into mutant udders. Yet the random dreams, the casually forgotten words, point elsewhere, strike me as inelegant and incomplete. Language supplies us with ways to express ever subtler levels of meaning, but does that imply language *gives* meaning, or robs us of it when we are at a loss to name things? I can think of several interpretations to ascribe to a girl who doesn't remember invoking the word *malignancy*, yet what do those theories have to do with me, who resists feeling anything other than bewilderment at the image of a child walking casually down a hall chanting agreeable, historyless words?

Sunday afternoons in the hospital were the stillest and longest — formless hours to be gotten through. With all the departments closed, there was none of the week's bustle. The familiar nurses were off, leaving us in the hands of unsympathetic aides who didn't care if we were entertained or not. In the stillness, the traffic on the street below sounded louder. There were more of the other patients' visitors to watch, obscure relatives who made the trip from out of town bearing useless flowers and ornately wrapped toys. But I grew tired of scrutinizing them, grew to recognize the swirling patterns and dynamics of every family that walked onto the ward complaining of how hard it was to park around here, how long the elevators took. Some older brother or father would find a surgical mask and put it on and laugh, believing he was the first to discover this antic. I'd sit on my bed looking for words hidden in a jumble of letters or vainly attempting to put together an incomplete jigsaw puzzle I'd found in the game room. The stiff sheets made the bottoms of my feet red, and I was always in trouble for not wearing my slippers when out of bed. A tart smell drifted down the hall from the sluice room, where they cleaned the bedpans and kept the sterilizer.

I could always count on Derek, who would appear beside me when I most needed him, decked out in his blue bathrobe with *Columbia Presbyterian* spelled out in fading black letters across the chest. There was one particular Sunday we'd been waiting for all week. Several days earlier we'd overheard a conversation between two of the staff nurses and a resident, something about the building where they kept the animals. Eavesdropping on adult conversations was something I did automatically, but the word animals pricked at me.

"They have animals here?" I interrupted.

"A whole floor of them, over in one of the other buildings. They try out new drugs and operations on them, to help humans."

I was very sensitive to being patronized, and I resented the tone in which this was said, but I was interested too. "How do you get there?"

The nurses and the doctor were all young and good-looking. Though couched in jargon, their conversations often held overtones of flirting, their true meanings as clear to me as a shiny present, unseen by the intended receiver, held cumbersomely behind the besotted one's back. I was probably annoying them.

"You have to go outside, across the street," the young doctor said.

"Aren't there tunnels to it?" a nurse asked.

"I guess so, but I've never been down there. I'm not even sure how you get to them."

Then they were off again, talking to each other, ignoring me, but it was too late. This was the adventure I'd been waiting for all my life. As I raced off to tell Derek, the doctor shouted at me to walk. Just to annoy them, I stopped short suddenly and surfed a good three feet along the well-polished floor on my socks.

Our main problem was that we didn't know how to get to the tunnels. Finally we were able to dupe a recently arrived teenaged candy striper into taking us, artfully making sure she didn't spill the beans to the nurses, who surely would have forbidden such an expedition. We convinced the candy striper that the nurses had said it was okay, and, just our luck, she even knew where the animal labs were because she used to work there as a messenger. She fell for it so perfectly that she even invited two of the other children to come along. Sunday was the brilliant choice because the regular staff, who were always suspicious of us, were off duty, and there was almost no chance of a doctor or technician coming to seek us out for some boring test.

This particular Sunday coincided with the first uncomfortably warm day of spring. All the windows were open, but they offered no relief. My T-shirt clung to my back as I slipped off the bed. Whenever possible, I dressed in street clothes. Wearing pajamas during the day, even though everyone else was wearing theirs, made me nervous and depressed. It brought to my mind the old practical joke of getting someone to show up in a chicken suit for a formal ball.

Once assembled in the hallway, Derek, the candy striper, the two other children, and I headed for the elevators. I knew there was a basement beneath the ground floor, but I didn't know there were levels even beneath that. Our bodies were transported through space to the very bottom, the terminus, SB2, subbasement level 2. The elevator doors opened on a long hallway with concrete walls, illuminated intermittently with bare light bulbs cradled in bell-shaped cages of wire dangling from the ceiling. It smelled cold. You could clearly see the imprints of the wood used as forms for the concrete, like vast slabs of petrified wood.

Derek leaned over and whispered in my ear, "This is where they keep the dead ones."

The notion that at any moment we might see a white-sheeted body being rolled down the hall made my fingers fall asleep. I shook them, bewildered by the effect. The candy striper walked forward authoritatively. But only fifty yards further, faced with an intersection, she faltered. We scanned the walls for signs pointing toward the building that housed the animal labs.

For days I'd been looking forward to this. Once or twice a year a traveling petting zoo was set up inside the local mall. For a small fee you could walk around the sawdust-filled pen and pet the obese goats and sheep. For an extra ten cents you could buy feed out of a converted bubblegum machine. I couldn't get enough of the animals, their smell, the clicks their cloven hooves made on the tile floor showing in patches through the sawdust. I was crazy for animals. Any book or television show or movie about animals I consumed greedily, though I shied away from the ones that anthropomorphized the animals. I thought it degraded them to be too closely aligned with the human species.

Uncharacteristically, Derek allowed me to walk in front of him. Normally there was a silent battle between us about who was in charge, but this morning he seemed distracted, or perhaps he wasn't as excited as I was. There were things about Derek I didn't understand; he could get sullen like this sometimes. Though I never would have admitted it to him, I envied the fact that he lived in the city year-round. I thought it made him exotic. Once I awakened to find him standing over me and two other boys peering in from the doorway: he'd kissed me. Perhaps they had wanted to watch, thinking I'd be grossed out, but my reaction obviously disappointed them. All I felt was somewhat confused as to why Derek, who looked equally confused, would want to do such a bizarre thing.

Eventually we found the tunnel that led to the correct building. We piled into the elevator and took it all the way up. The doors opened onto a large foyer. Open windows with spectacular views of the city took up most of two walls. A cool, strong wind came through the windows, whose unbarred expanses struck me as dangerous. With the unpainted ceiling and concrete floors, they gave the place a tenuous feeling. On either side of the foyer were sets of swinging doors. We went through one set and down a hallway, realized it was wrong, turned back, and went through the foyer again. As we opened the second set of doors the stink hit us head on. The tang of natural urea and ammonia mixed with the chemical fumes of disinfectants burned the inside of my nose. This probably should have been an omen, but we continued on down the hall, following the smell, until we saw the doors: *Authorized Personnel Only.* There wasn't an authorized human in sight.

We pushed open the doors and found ourselves in a large room. Equipment of various sorts lined the walls, and in the middle stood four interlocking pens with metal poles for sides. In two of the pens were pigs, and in the other two, sheep. They had no bedding, and the concrete floor, dribbled with urine, sloped downward toward a system of drains. My first thought was, how can they sleep on concrete? The animals had been lying down, but our entrance startled them. They stood up, the sheep bleating hoarsely and the pigs harumphing, very human-sounding, and circled the tight interior of their pens. I'd never been so close to pigs before, and these were enormous. Pigs have human eyes, blue, with round pupils. After staring at you they look away, and you can see the whites of their eyes. Counter to every feeling I'd ever had about an animal before, I had no desire to go nearer.

We all just stood there in the doorway. Surely things were said, but I don't remember any conversation. As the sheep paced around I noticed that patches of fleece had been shaved away in raw geometrics, framed for recently sutured incisions. One of the sheep had what looked like a plastic bag sewn into her side. We stepped back out and went into the next room, where dogs had started barking. Half a dozen beagles in reasonably large cages greeted us joyously. One of the dogs looked unhappy and sick and ignored us, but the rest pushed with all their weight against their bars as we approached. As I neared the first one's cage, however, he stopped barking and growled at me. The candy striper heard and warned me not to get any closer to the dogs, most of whom looked desperate for attention. All of a sudden I hated her, with her stupid outfit and shrill, silly voice.

Desperation saturated the room in those loud, whining cries pacing back and forth, back and forth, back and forth. I was overwhelmed. On each cage door was a sign with handwritten details about the dog, filled with alien words. Instead of water dishes they had bottles with tubes they could lick, giant versions of what my gerbils used back home. Despite the warning, I let the dogs lick my fingers through the bars.

The tenor of the expedition was shifting rapidly, taking on a slow, almost viscous quality. Our teenaged grownup tried to hurry us along, now aware that she'd made a mistake. The next room was lined with cages. The wall directly across from the door was filled with cages of white mice, and to our right was an entire wall of cats, cage after cage stacked upon each other. Most were tabbies. I'd never seen so many cats in one place, and yet it was eerily silent. They crouched in their cages and stared at us, every single one of them, as we filed into the room. As we got closer, some of them came up to the bars of their cages and rubbed, opening their mouths soundlessly. Years later I learned that it is not uncommon to cut the vocal cords of laboratory cats, especially if there are a lot of them. They had the same water bottles and handwritten signs as the beagles, but their cages were smaller. A number of the cats had matchbox-size rectangles with electrical wires implanted in their skulls. The skin on their shaved scalps was crusty and red where it joined the metal.

It was too much now. There was a sound of monkeys in

the next room, but we turned and left. In the elevator no one spoke; in the tunnels no one spoke. A sad, groping presence accompanied us all the way back to the ward, where the lunch trays were just arriving and the aroma of spaghetti filled the halls. When asked where we'd been, our candy striper replied casually that we'd gone for a walk, and not one of us said anything to the contrary. Sooner or later we all have to learn the words with which to name our own private losses, but then we just stood there in front of the nurses' desk, speechless.

THREE

The Tao of Laugh-In

∽

NO ONE CLEARLY EXPLAINED TO ME WHAT WAS about to happen. Mary, the head nurse, did call me over at one point. Derek tagged along. The floors had just been polished, and the lemon scent of wax filled the air. Mary was one of my favorite nurses, always kind and always the one most likely to crack a joke as she walked into the room with that dreaded basin, the one they carried needles in. Though I didn't mind blood tests, I'd developed a fear of preop injections.

By now I'd had three operations, including a bone biopsy. Usually they gave two injections before taking you down to the O.R., one for each thigh, and the shots hurt like bad leg cramps for several minutes. Most nurses offered the hearty and useless advice of *Rub that spot hard!* or *Squeeze your toes!*, but not Mary. She'd stand over you, needle poised, and announce her own joking version of comfort, mimicking the syrupy tone neophyte inflicters commonly resort to: *Now this isn't going to hurt me one little bit.*

I specifically asked Mary if she'd give me the injection before my fourth operation, the one that involved removing the tumor and no more than one third of the jaw. She seemed disappointed when she told me that she wouldn't be on duty for it. Late that afternoon, before she left, she called me over. "This is a big operation you'll have tomorrow, you know that, don't you?"

I'd been told it would take a whole four hours, which was certain to elevate my social status on the ward. Though I'd felt sick after my other encounters with anesthetics, I didn't comprehend what a four-hour surgery would mean. Somewhat chagrined at being spoken down to, I told her I understood everything perfectly, unaware that I hadn't a clue how sick I was or what was going to happen.

She looked me right in the eye. "Do you know you'll look different afterward?"

For Derek's sake, I made a joke about bandages, about looking like The Mummy. Horror movies were a major source of entertainment for Derek and me. Between us we'd seen every bad monster movie ever made, and we had serious arguments as to whether or not Camera, a giant Japanese turtle, could win over Rodin, another Japanese creature with a pterodactyl look. Mary realized she wasn't getting anywhere with me. She shifted her weight, looked down, and let her shoe slip halfway off her foot to dangle on the edge of her toes. After a few moments of contemplating this effect, she put her weight back on the foot. I could hear the stockings rasp together on her thighs as she left.

The next afternoon, when I woke up in Recovery, I

couldn't quite figure out where I was or what had happened to me. My entire body ached, and when I tried to speak, nothing happened. An elderly, overweight nurse approached my head from time to time with a long, clear plastic tube, which seemed to disappear just as a deep ache appeared in my lungs. I didn't realize I had had a tracheotomy. There was a constant loud sound of machines, and at one point I amused the nurses, who showed me how to speak by placing a finger over the hole in my throat, by asking if they could turn them off so I could get some decent sleep. My parents came in together for a minute, stood at the foot of the bed, and considered me from what seemed a long, long way away.

With no room in ICU, they decided to keep me overnight in Recovery. I held my hand over my throat, over my newest orifice, and felt my breath brush warm, almost hot, over the moist plane of my palm. The steady flutter didn't seem to have anything to do with me. For the first few hours I vomited up large amounts of blood I'd swallowed during the procedure. I began to welcome the deep, lungy urge to release the sweet-tasting fluid from deep within me. It tasted almost pleasant. Drainage tubes drifted down onto the pillow beside me, displaying the slightly shifting red and golden fluids of my body. An IV hung over me, dripping steadily and endlessly, producing a hypnotic effect similar to that of the watery chaos I'd been drawn to off the stern of the *Queen Mary*. If I lay perfectly still, I felt no pain. I dozed and woke, dozed and woke all night, slept my half-sleep with an image of myself as swaddled.

* * *

Bizarrely, after they removed half my jaw, I limped. It was my first day up out of bed, and I was going to traverse the entire four feet to the bathroom. This required a certain amount of preparation, of disconnecting tubes and wires.

"Why are you limping? They didn't do anything to your legs, Chicken-chops."

My mother was watching the nurse help me. I liked it when she called me Chicken-chops, the name she used with any of us when we were ill. I was back on Ward 10, not only in my own room but with my own nurses around the clock. Most of them simply sat beside my bed and read, but the one that day liked to turn the television on without volume and chuckle at it continuously. Underdog wavered on the screen behind my mother as she put down her knitting to view the spectacle of my first journey out of bed. I placed my finger over my throat.

"I don't know."

It was everything I could do just to say those three words. My non sequitur limping seemed to amuse the nurse and my mother, and eventually it amused me. None of us understood that the body is a connected thing.

Fluid was the major issue. I refused to drink enough. Or, rather, that's how they perceived my inability to down more than a quarter of a glass at a time. Every swallow left me breathless, two swallows exhausted me, three and then four made me feel I should be congratulated. Instead they made an embarrassing chart and pinned it on the door, a Magic Marker record of every cc I consumed. They thought the threats to never take out my IV would impel me, but they misjudged. I gladly would have spent the rest of my life on an IV if they would just leave me alone.

Day after day passed, and still I could barely manage a fraction of the ten glasses a day they wanted of me. Ten glasses! An unimaginable sum! Couldn't they see that? I knew my mother was getting annoyed with me, beginning to take it personally. How could I explain that I just wanted to lie there, becoming ever more intimate with my body?

I knew all of my body's rhythms now, all of its quirks. The smell of my wound was sweet and ever-present, the skin on my elbows and heels as sore and red as holly berries. Though at first I'd dreaded the daily injections, now I didn't even mind them, welcomed the dozy contentedness they offered. I learned that all I had to do was relax, that fear was the worst part. I became a machine for disassembling fear. Even the worst pains could be rendered harmless if you relaxed into them, didn't fight. I grew lazy about speaking, and even after I was given a full-time plug for my trachea, I put little effort into speaking, reducing my vocabulary to only syllables at a time, passing them out as cautiously as I did my attempts to drink the most minute amounts of water. I grew weaker and weaker.

They started feeding me through a gastronasal tube, which had been inserted earlier. Each mealtime a tray arrived with my name on it, a tray filled with liquidated *everything,* even turkey. I asked them to let me smell each container before they poured it into the tube. Aroma alone started to revive me. I could feel the hot or cold of the liquid pass through my nose and the back of my throat.

Finally, at about five in the morning of my tenth birthday,
I tricked a nurse into giving me some orange Jell-O. It was
the first thing I'd eaten in a week, and instantly I felt better,
began to see that this bed wasn't a continuous state, that
one day, one way or another, I would feel better.

When my whole family came to visit me for my birthday, I sat in a wheelchair and gazed at them, feeling splen-
did. I could tell they were shocked at the sight of me. I had
been an absolutely normal nine-year-old the last time they
saw me, some ten days before. My older sister spoke politely to me, as did my twin sister. They'd never been polite
to me before, and I knew that a chasm had opened between us. How could I explain that the way I felt now was
actually *better?* How could they ever know where I had just
come from? Suddenly I understood the term *visiting.* I was
in one place, they were in another, and they were only
pausing. We made polite conversation about people at
school, from the neighborhood, talked about things entirely inconsequential because it wasn't the subject that
counted but the gesture of conversation itself. You could
have parsed each sentence not into nouns and verbs but
into signs and symbols, artificial reports from a buffer zone
none of us really owned or cared to inhabit.

My mother was the Visitor Extraordinaire. She'd arrive
each afternoon, give me whatever bit of news or information about my health she had as quickly and simply as
possible, then sit down in a chair and begin knitting. She'd
spend the entire visit knitting. Human presence is the
important part of visiting, and she understood that. Her

body occupied a space close to my body, but it didn't ask anything of it. Other visitors were more awkward — casual friends of the family who'd stop by and stand over me for long and clumsy minutes, trying to engage me in conversation, when all I wanted was for them to sit down, relax, not say a word.

My father was the worst visitor. He loved puns and would think of a more terrible one each day. But in the awkward silence that followed his rehearsed routine, what should he do then? Sometimes he'd put on a surgical mask and make a joke about Dr. Dad, the same joke I'd seen dozens of other fathers make with their kids. Then, bereft of a vector, he'd sit down and stare intently at the drip of my IV. He could sit like that for a long time, personally coaxing each drop to form and fall. I knew how hard it was for him, and he probably knew how hard it was for me.

On certain afternoons after that first big operation and in later years, I would recognize my father's particular gait far down the hall. He'd come on his lunch break, though he didn't have much time to visit, with his hectic work schedule. We both knew that his visits were slow and sorrowful for both of us and that it was okay for him to come only occasionally. One day I heard his step echoing toward me. Carefully, still not entirely sure what I was intending, I got into bed and closed my eyes. His loud breathing and hard-soled shoes entered the room. Silence stood over me for a minute or two, contemplating. I heard hands fumble around in coat pockets for a minute, the crinkle of paper, a pen covering it with soft thips of sound. Then at once everything was leaving the room, pulling out of it and leaving behind that specific, hollow sound of emptiness. I opened my eyes and read the note I found on my night table. "Lucy, I was here but you were sound asleep. I didn't want to wake you. Love, Daddy." I felt I'd let us both off the hook, yet after that the afternoon seemed interminable, something to be gotten through.

Gradually I began to improve. I gained strength, the various tubes were removed, and walking became less of a heroic effort. I still resisted speaking, however, keeping my answers to a simple yes or no when I could not just nod my head. I allowed people to believe speaking was difficult, though my mother knew better and kept at me constantly. One day Mary came in when I was alone and announced very casually that I was much better now, that someone else needed this room and, because there were no beds on this ward, I was to be transferred to the floor above. She left as casually as she had come. It was the first day I'd gotten dressed in regular clothes, a Spiderman shirt someone had brought as a present. A feeling of regret came over me. Perhaps if I hadn't gotten dressed they would still think I was sick enough to stay. A few minutes later an aide came in to help me pack. I excused myself and went into the bathroom, where I was overcome by weeping, the first tears I'd shed since I'd been in the hospital.

How could they throw me out like this? I had come to believe that the nurses there liked me, that they were my special friends, yet now I was just being tossed away. Only then did I begin to realize how accustomed I'd grown to being taken care of. I hadn't even had to wash myself. And as much as I hated to concede any points to my mother, I knew I had become too passive. An ornate surge of grief came over me, too manifold for me to know what I was grieving for. Luckily I tired easily, and the weeping could go on for only a few moments. I wiped my eyes. Ashamed of myself, I went back into the room to help the aide gather my things into a red plastic disposal bag with WARNING: HAZARDOUS WASTE written in large black letters across it. My mother had taken my overnight case home early on because it took up too much room.

The new ward was laid out exactly like Ward 10, but it was filled with a different kind of patient. These were teenaged girls who giggled with each other and told jokes that I didn't get about the doctors, especially one Dr. Silverman, whom they all seemed to be in love with. One girl with long black hair and lovely dark eyes sang his name over and over again in a voice I told her was good enough to be on the radio. She looked pleased when I told her this. All of them were skeletally thin; knowing nothing of anorexia, I wondered what was wrong with them. There were no visible scars or signs of illness that I could see, apart from their weight. One of them was so thin she couldn't walk, and the others pushed her about in a wheelchair. Her arms were so thin that her elbows looked like giant swollen lumps, her hands like the oversized hands of someone who has worked long and hard for a lifetime. Though they were older than me, having already entered that mysterious, enviable realm of the teenager, they wore toddler-sized name bands, the only ones small enough to fit their delicate and fragile wrists.

I spent a week on the new ward, but I never committed

to making friends there. Derek came up to see me once or twice, but then he too was discharged. My body started orienting itself toward home, feeling stronger and more bored every day. I still had sticky circles on my chest, remnants of the EKG, and my fingertips were covered with small black marks, scars from the daily blood tests, but my body was my own once more. Though I had looked at the scar running down the side of my still swollen face, it hadn't occurred to me to scrutinize how I *looked*. I was missing a section of my jaw, but the extreme swelling, which stayed with me for two months, hid the defect. Before the operation I hadn't had a strong sense of what I looked like anyway. Proud of my tomboy heritage, I'd dogmatically scorned any attempts to look pretty or girlish. A classmate named Karen had once told me I was beautiful, and by the third grade two boys had asked me to be their girlfriend, all of which bewildered me. When Derek had delivered my first actual kiss, his desire had taken me completely by surprise. On the day I finally went home, I felt only proud of my new, dramatic scar and eager to show it off.

School was already over for the year. The endlessness of summer stretched out before me, temptingly narcotic. I wasn't allowed to go swimming because the scar on my trachea was still soft and fresh, a pink button on my throat, but I didn't really mind. I was a hero. Neighbors stopped me on the heat-rippled sidewalks to ask how I was. Evan, my closest friend from the neighborhood, and the other boys seemed suitably impressed with my hospital tales

(I embellished heartily) and with my coup: I didn't have to make up any of the two months of schoolwork I'd missed.

One afternoon when Evan and I were playing an intricate game of jungle in his living room, his father passed through on his way to the kitchen. Pausing in the doorway for a moment, he turned and addressed me directly. I knew that his wife had died of cancer several years before, but I couldn't have imagined what went through his mind to now see a child with the same disease, the same prospects. He was the first person to mention chemotherapy, and he looked at me steadily and sadly for a minute before asking if I knew what it was. I'd been told I was going to have chemotherapy, but it had been described as simply another drug, another injection, maybe one that would make me a little flushed, no more. I'd had some unpleasant scans involving injected dyes, which had transformed the world into something woozy and hot, but nothing so bad that I felt unable to face it again.

My explanation wasn't what he was expecting, but, unable or unwilling to finish what he'd started, he mentioned something vague about chemical changes in my body, about how my hair might be affected. Having no idea what he was talking about and sensing something serious I'd rather not pursue, I made a joke to Evan about how my hair would turn green, my eyes purple. This was the second time an adult had tried to approach me directly and seriously about my situation, and it was the second time I had turned it around, refused to tackle it.

* * *

Death had become part of my vocabulary when I was six. The gerbil was the latest in a long line of family pets to die, and with my sister Susie, who was twelve at the time, I was disposing of the body behind the house. Our dog Cassie had died a year or so before, and though I missed her, at the time I had felt confused by Susie's irrational tears and bad tempers in the days afterward. Now the gerbil was also dead, and though I'd had no real attachment to him, I was sorry. He lay on top of a brown paper bag from the A&P, soon to be his final shroud. His fur parted and clumped together in a strange way, the deadest thing about him, and when I touched him I couldn't believe how hard, how cold, he was. Susie picked him up by his tail, and the sunlight suddenly illuminated the dullness of his still open eyes. A strange idea entered my head, an idea so preposterous it couldn't be true. How could it be? Surely Susie would laugh at me for even suggesting it, but I felt I had to make sure anyway, for my own peace of mind.

I paused for a moment, considering how best to phrase it. I went for the negative approach.

"People don't die, do they?"

She looked at me with the surprise I'd hoped for, the faintly amused look that told me my fear was unfounded, but her response became proof positive that one should never ask a twelve-year-old sister *anything*. With glee in her voice she commenced to describe in great detail how you went into the cold dark ground, how the skin fell off your bones, how your eyes fell out. In a truly inspired touch, she began singing:

The worms crawl in, the worms crawl out,
in your stomach and out your mouth.

I don't blame her. I was an easy mark, and had I been in her position I'd have done the same thing. Part of the job of being human is to consistently underestimate our effect on other people, and for the specific job of being a twelve-year-old with a younger sister, cruelty is de rigueur.

As we stood there near the driveway, Susie had no idea what she had just implanted in the deepest part of me. No one had any idea, not my parents or teachers or friends, because there was no way I could discuss it. If the word *death* was even mentioned in my presence, I would collapse. At night I dreamed of being carted off and left alone in a dark, cold room filled with bones, bones that would wake up once I was in there and dance around me. There was a small, dark hole in the steps in front of our house that led nowhere in particular, but in my new dreams it became the gateway to a world that terrified me, a world where people had no heads or, if they did, they were filled with worms and beetles. This was what awaited me, there was no way I was going to escape death, and as the days passed I became more and more frantic. If I saw a movie or television show that involved someone's death, I'd hide under the covers. When a schoolmate I didn't even know died tragically in a fire, I was convinced that I was somehow responsible.

Why had we been born if this was the terrible end we had to look forward to? My six-year-old self was privately obsessed with my terrors and questions, when salvation appeared in the most surprising place — the television show *Laugh-In*. A repeating skit, mixed in with all the sexual and political innuendos that were over my head, was the scenario of a ragged, exhausted man climbing to the top of a large mountain. At the peak sat a man with a long gray beard. The climber would ask the guru, "Oh master, what is the meaning of life?" Of course the answer was always a silly one, usually resulting in the climber's falling off the mountain. I'd seen references to a similar mountain and guru in the cartoon "B.C." Then I saw a National Geographic program that located this mountain, with its guru, in an actual place called Tibet. Immediately I went to my father. He was sitting in the living room, reading on the red couch so accustomed to his body that it obligingly hollowed to hold him more comfortably. After his death I used to curl up into this space and lie there with the cats, the warmth of his physical dent as reassuring as some ghostly hand in my hair.

"Daddy, how much would a plane ticket to Tibet cost?" I asked, offering no explanation for my question.

His eyes went up into his head and he scrunched up his forehead to let me know he was thinking. Looking down at his palm, he pretended to do calculations, muttering to himself. After a minute of this he turned and looked at me as he would an adult. "One million dollars," he announced, as seriously as I had asked him. I thanked him and left. For a six-year-old, one million dollars was about as unintelligible as one hundred, but I decided to start saving. I understood it might take some time, possibly years.

Gradually my obsession with death was replaced with other obsessions, with new, daily discoveries about what it meant to be alive. But for a long time I put myself to sleep at night by imagining the mountain, the long, arduous climb. I counted off each step the way other people counted sheep, and each night that I made it to the top I'd ask my question, yearning to hear every minute answering vibration of sound, believing that perfecting my ability to listen was all I needed to know the answer. Truth was something that existed; it's just that it lived far away.

I had long forgotten the trauma of the gerbil when I became ill, and the idea that death had anything to do with me directly didn't even enter my mind. It wasn't so much avoidance but the simple belief that nothing bad would ever, *could* ever, happen to me. Sometimes I wonder if it wasn't this disbelief that kept me alive. Even later, when I could not avoid realizing that I was very ill, I didn't understand that what was happening to me was important, dangerous. Despite my knowing that people died, it never occurred to me that I might personally be implicated.

Later, as a teenager, I worked in a library, and one day as I was reshelving books I found myself in the medical section, where a book on pediatric oncology caught my eye. Pulling the heavy thing out, I laid it on the table, opened to the index, and looked up my cancer, Ewing's sarcoma. I turned to the given page and read a brief description of the various manifestations of it, followed by a table of mortality rates. A reasonable chance of survival was given at five percent.

The paper of the book was heavy and almost cream-colored, and I ran my finger along the letters, which were so black I half expected to feel them raised up on the page. I looked up. The room was empty and buzzing with both bad light and the numerous stacks of books I still had to shelve. *Five percent.* I felt obliged to say something, but no one was there, and I didn't know what I was supposed to say anyway. Placing my hand on my neck, feeling the pulse there, I stood for some minutes on the verge of moving or speaking or sitting or *something.* Then the impulse passed, and I was on the other side of it, feeling as if I'd forgotten something, some name or object or emotion I'd meant to take note of but had carelessly allowed to slip by. Finally someone walked into the room, breaking the silence with the squeak of winter boots, and I turned, reaching for another book to shelve.

FOUR

Fear Itself

⌐

THE STREETS IN NEW YORK CITY ARE THEIR OWN country. A knowledge of them gives one a sense of power. It makes no difference that for the most part New York is a giant grid, supremely traversable compared with such labyrinths as Paris or London. Its power heaves up from the pavement right in front of your eyes, steam escapes in fits and starts as if the whole place were going to blow any minute, people who have already blown apart lie crumpled in its crevasses, and all the while there is a thin promise, a slight wheedling tone, that something important, something drastic, is about to break.

I drove with my mother into the city five days a week, every week, for two years for radiation and chemotherapy treatments, and then once a week for another half year to finish out the chemotherapy, which was administered most Fridays, with periodic "vacations." My mother worked mornings in a local nursing home and would come to pick me up at our house at midday. We got into the car in our suburb, drove for just under an hour through the relative countryside of the Palisades Parkway, propelled ourselves across the Hudson via the George Washington Bridge, and found ourselves deposited smack in the middle of another world. Billboards advertised the good life in Spanish, ancient cobblestones emerged in patches from the tar, which shivered and smelled in summer and shone black and cruel in the winter. Grotesque figures loomed everywhere, but they didn't frighten me, nor did the filthy and the slobbering insane, the homeless and the drunk. I felt keenly the great expanses, the chasmal spaces between all of us, which one seemed prepared to reach across. Even as I was spooked, I was impressed by and admiring of the constant chord of toughness and strength, which acted to harmonize all the many and varied notes in the city, the thousand and one vignettes of overheard conversations, glimpsed lives.

My mother and I usually drove the miles to the city engulfed by our own private, inner travels, the radio's sound filling the front seat like an anesthetic. Once we got to the city and went through the customary parking ordeal, we walked the few blocks to the hospital in silence. This was the routine we fell into, and it seemed natural to both of us.

The Radiotherapy Department existed deep in the guts of the hospital in a specially built section with cement walls many feet thick. Chris, my "radiotherapist," explained that careful regulations made the walls so thick. She placed her hand on the otherwise innocuous, pale yellow plaster and told me in reverent tones about the care one had to take around radiation. She herself wore a thick green smock made of lead. She let me hold it once, and it seemed to weigh as much as I did.

On my first visit I could tell Chris was keen for me to see her "as a friend." Her hair was streaked blond and her arms were strong and athletic. Her uniform was an unbecoming yellow that clashed with the yellow walls. The entire department had a different feel from the rest of the hospital, set off by a cocoon quality and by genuine attempts to make something human of this lead and cement hole in the ground. The employees hung up family photos on the reception area walls, and if they didn't have kids of their own, they put up overly cute pictures of cats and dogs. Posters of orangutans proclaiming *Every time I figure out the rules, they change them* and of puppies thanking God it was Friday adorned the ceilings of the treatment rooms, demanding attention as I lay on my back.

Radiation treatment itself was a breeze, about as complicated as an x-ray. I'd get up on the table, and Chris would don her lead smock and turn out the lights. Bulbs inside the clunky machine hanging from tracks on the ceiling would shine down on my face, waiting to be aligned with the Magic Marker x's drawn on my neck and face. "Hold your breath!" the command would come from somewhere in the corner, and I'd inhale as deeply as I could, almost always thinking about a movie I'd seen, a maritime disaster in which the hero had to swim a long distance underwater in order to save everyone else. I'd held my breath along with him, wondering if I too had it in me to save the others. Believing that one should be prepared for any emergency, I went about trying to improve my breath-holding capacity, and lying there on the gurney in Radiotherapy seemed as good a place as any to practice for a disaster at sea. As the machines over my head clicked and whirred softly, my body swelled with air, trembling almost imperceptibly with the desire to let it all fall away from me, deflate back out to the place it had come from. Just when I was about to abandon all hope and let the salty water fill my lungs, Chris's voice would sound from the dark corner.

"Breathe!" The overhead lights came on, Chris appeared without her lead burden and helped me off the table, and it was all over until the next day.

If it was Monday, Tuesday, Wednesday, or Thursday, that was the whole procedure. I'd find my mother in the waiting room, and we'd take the long elevator ride back up to street level, get back in the car, and head home, hoping to avoid rush-hour traffic. Friday was different. Every Friday, usually around three o'clock, was my appointment with Dr. Woolf at the chemotherapy clinic.

I was already two weeks into the radiation treatment before I had my first appointment with Dr. Woolf, and despite Evan's father's early warning attempts, I went into it completely unprepared. Radiation at that point seemed like a good deal — all that time off from school, no pain, or at least not yet, the meditative drives into the city with my mother. The only thing that really worried me about chemo was the prospect of weekly injections, because that's all I thought it would be, an injection. If I had been blind to what the original operation would be like, and blind to warnings about chemo, once I entered the clinic I got my first intimations of what was about to happen.

In sharp contrast to the new Radiotherapy Department, the chemotherapy clinic was old-looking, drab. The main waiting area was on one side of a much-used hall, a main thoroughfare for the hospital. It was completely open, like a lounge, and on the walls hung dark oil portraits of men whose names I never bothered to learn. The couches and chairs were covered in dark green vinyl, the floor was black tile with white traces almost worn out of existence. My mother wasn't allowed to smoke, which drove her insane, especially since week after week for two and a half years we had to wait at least two hours past the scheduled time before my name was called.

The other people in the waiting room fascinated me. We all looked exhausted, though relative health seemed to vary widely. Over the years I became expert at diagnosing the drugs each child was receiving from his or her appearance. Some looked bloated and sluggish, others were thin as rakes, and almost everyone was in some stage of losing or growing in their hair. Hats, scarves, and wigs covered the naked scalps. On that first visit I felt apart from the rest of them, felt a million miles away.

When we were finally in Dr. Woolf's office, my mother ready to scream from the long wait, we encountered his telephone, apparently a permanent appendage. He could carry on a conversation with my mother, me, his nurse, his secretary down the hall, and someone on the phone simultaneously; he had it down to an art. My mother thought him incredibly rude, and she was right. Dr. Woolf's man-

ner was gruff and unempathetic. The first time he examined me I could only flinch at his roughness as his large
fingers pressed hard into my abdomen, pried open my still
stiff mouth. His appearance didn't help. Tall, large-fea-
tured, and balding, he had a peculiar large white spot on
his forehead, which caught the light in an unflattering,
sinister way. His nose was tremendous, his lips invisible.
He scared me.

His office was as drab as the waiting room but was saved
by a large, multipaned window that looked out onto a
well-tended courtyard with banks of blue flowers and ivy-
clenched trees. I spent a lot of time looking out that window. I spent a lot of time forcing myself to look out that
window, because even on that first visit I knew that this
room was no place for me. The only thing I wanted to
know about this particular interior was its implicit exte-
rior, an existence that had nothing to do with me, Dr.
Woolf, my mother, the treatment table, which was too tall
for me to get onto by myself, or the two 60-cc syringes
waiting patiently in their sterile packets.

This first examination was more thorough than the
ones I would later receive. I was asked to strip down to my
underwear, which I did, feeling humiliated and exposed.
While the doctor talked to the nurse, my mother, and the
person on the phone tucked beneath his chin, he prodded
me with his hands, hit me just slightly too hard with his
reflex hammer, and spoke far too loudly. When he touched
me I could feel the vibrations of his voice in my own chest,
feel them lapsing through my body's cavity the same way
you feel a car passing too closely. He got out a tourniquet

and wound it tightly around my arm, pinching the skin just like a kid on the playground giving an Indian burn, and despite every ounce of strength I could muster, I began to cry. Not loudly, not even particularly heartily, just a few simple tears, which were as accurate and prophetic as any I'd ever shed.

The butterfly needle, named for the winglike holds that fanned out from its short, delicate, bodylike cylinder, slipped into my arm, a slender pinch I barely felt. Because it was inserted into the crook of my arm, I had to sit with my arm rigidly straight, held up awkwardly and overly self-consciously. I began to grow warm, a caustic ache began settling into my elbow. For a split second, a split of a split second, the sensation was almost pleasurable, a glowing, fleshy sense of my body recognizing itself as a body, a thing in the world. But immediately it was too much: I felt the lining of my stomach arc out and pull spastically back into itself like some colorful disturbed sea anemone.

It was an anatomy lesson. I had never known it was possible to *feel* your organs, feel them the way you feel your tongue in your mouth, or your teeth. My stomach outlined itself for me; my intestines, my liver, parts of me I didn't know the names of began heating up, trembling with their own warmth, creating friction and space by rubbing against the viscera, the muscles of my stomach, my back, my lungs. I wanted to collapse, to fall back onto the table or, better yet, go head first down onto the cold floor, but I couldn't. The injection had only begun; this syringe was still half full and there was a second one to go. My head began to hurt. Not sure if my brain was shrinking or swelling, I squinted around the office, not in the least bit surprised to see a yellow-green aura surrounding everyone, everything, like some macabre religious painting.

My body, wanting to turn itself inside out, made wave after wave of attempts to rid itself of this unseeable intruder, this overwhelming and noxious poison. I shook with heaves so strong they felt more like convulsions. Someone lifted a metal basin to my face, and I quickly deposited in it everything my digestive system owned, and when that wasn't enough I came up with the digestive juices themselves, pitiful spoonfuls of green bile, and then I just threw up air, breathing it down in deep gasps between bucking it back up in spasms that ached with fruitlessness. It was the emptiness that hurt the most. When my stomach had something to offer back it was happy to do so, but when it was empty, the convulsions still came, my stomach pressing inward with even greater self-spite, punishing its own lack by squeezing ever harder.

Gradually the waves of vomiting subsided, leaving behind an unacted-upon nausea that seemed to involve not just my stomach but all of me, even my feet, my scalp. As a result of the vomiting my sinuses swelled and ached, but knowing nothing about sinuses, I could only report that my nose hurt. Dr. Woolf looked puzzled but didn't follow up with any further questions. Someone helped me put my clothes back on; I don't remember the walk back to the car.

The sky was so blue it was almost transparent, and it moved seamlessly outside the window as I lay in the back seat. The trip home was straightforward, from the bridge onto the parkway, then off the parkway, down a few streets, and up the driveway. Once we were off the bridge, it was a half-hour trip, and I calculated there were only nine turns from start to finish. From this unfamiliar vantage point, without the normal visual landmarks, I stared at the sky and attempted to guess where we were. Each time the car turned I tried to visualize what it was turning toward: Exit 14, the supermarket, the stone house on the corner, our house. Somewhere along the way I messed up. I thought we were at least two more turns away, but suddenly I felt the rise of the driveway and knew I was wrong, but it would be the last time. Over the years I perfected the mental drive, could do it even when I was half asleep, even when the rhythm was interrupted by a sudden need to vomit into the kitchen mixing bowl my mother placed on the floor.

That first time I arrived home I remember feeling not quite so bad. I'd begun to feel less nauseous, or at least better able to control it. My father suggested I eat something, some ice cream perhaps. My head swimming, I sat at the kitchen table and ate several spoonfuls, my parents looking at me expectantly.

"It wasn't so bad, was it now, Lucinda Mag?" my father asked.

I shook my head no, purposefully bringing another spoonful of the vanilla, chocolate, and strawberry mixture up to my mouth. Speaking seemed like something one could grow tired of.

My stomach rebelled. I stood quickly and made my way over to the sink, where I threw up the now liquid ice cream, still cool and even soothing as it came up. For some reason I started to cry. My mother put her hand on my head and tried to soothe me, and when I was done began to explain that there was no need to cry, that everything would be all right, that I mustn't cry.

How could she know I would take her so seriously? She went on to explain how disappointed she was that I'd cried even before Dr. Woolf had put the needle into me, that crying was only because of fear, that I shouldn't be afraid, it would be all right. It was one thing to cry afterward, because she knew that it hurt, but why did I cry before-hand? Hadn't I always been so brave before?

I looked out the kitchen window over the sink I had just thrown up into. Straggles of spider-plant cuttings had taken over most of it, the brown, tangled roots filling an assortment of drinking glasses placed on the ledges. There was also a collection of small ceramic houses, presents and mementos accumulated over the years. Immediately out-side, the overgrown, sloppy fir trees prevented any clear view of the front lawn or street.

Sometimes the briefest moments capture us, force us to take them in, and demand that we live the rest of our lives in reference to them. What did my mother mean? Part of me knew then, and still knows, that she was afraid for me. If somehow she could convince me not to be afraid, we could rally around the truism she had grown up with: there was nothing to fear but fear itself. My mother didn't know how to conquer *what* I was afraid of, nor could she even begin to tell me how to do it for myself. Instead, out of her own fear, she offered her own philosophy, which meant in this instance that I should conquer the fear by not crying. It was a single brief sentence, a fleeting thought she probably did not mean and doesn't even remember saying but I, who would have done anything to find a way out of this pain, would never forget it. As I made my way downstairs to my room, I resolved to never cry again.

I kept my bedroom dark and watched the light from my television change color on the wall beside me. Every hour or so I felt a great urge to lean over and retch into the mixing bowl on the floor. I drank water constantly so as to have something to throw up. As soon as the vomiting was over I'd feel whole continents better, and the intense nausea that had been unendurable only moments before was suddenly bearable, exposed as a fake, something I'd only mistakenly thought I could not bear a second longer. I'd lie back on the pillow feeling both energized and exhausted. Gradually, over the next hour, the feeling of unbearableness would return, subtly, insidiously, until I again had to lift myself up and hang over the side of the bed, my intimate bowl beneath me. This went on all night.

The second day was better. The cycle between nausea and relief would gradually extend so that I was throwing up only every four hours, every six hours, only three times during the night. The third day was the breaking point. I could actually eat something innocuous like tapioca. I quickly learned to judge food not by what it tasted like in eating but how it tasted when I threw it back up. Vanilla pudding was best, though it turned an unfortunate color, making me opt for chocolate for purely aesthetic reasons. I'd try to leave it down long enough so that I could digest most, possibly even all, of it before my stomach rebelled yet again.

Sometime during the late afternoon, relief would come. A flicker at first, only a moment, but for that brief moment I understood I was going to get better, that this was going to end. I sat up in bed, felt the strength of my body support me. Another moment would go by and I'd feel ill again, my head beginning to throb, but an hour, maybe two hours later, the feeling would return, stay for just a few breaths longer before abandoning me. The next period of illness would be a few shades briefer, and so it would go on through the evening. When I woke up on the fourth day I felt only a little weak, a little washed out, but glorious and high, that sanguine, comfortable feeling one gets after performing some great physical feat. I had swum the Channel. I had climbed Mount Eiger.

I sat up, listening for the sounds of my mother's foot-steps, the clicking of the dog's nails on the tiled floor. A tree obscured my window, shattering the light into patches on the dirty glass. I didn't understand how I could have overlooked the sheer joy of these things for so long, how the intricate message of their simplicity had escaped me until just this moment. This weightless now-ness, this ecstasy could sometimes last me all day, at least until that afternoon, when it was time to go back to the hospital for the radiation treatment, which, as I've said, didn't seem so bad, not really, anyway.

The fifth day was Tuesday, my favorite day of all. All but completely recovered, yet excused from the burden of school, I was free to wander about the still house, form intimate relationships with the cats and dogs, who regarded me nonjudgmentally as I tracked their movements over the living room floor, sleepily following the inexorable arc of the sun. Tuesday, still far away from Friday, was futureless, thoughtless, anxiety-free.

The house itself mothered me. With everyone else away at school or at work, I somehow thought my eavesdropping created a new meaning for the clock, the hot water heater, the cats growling over their food. I felt that my listening made for them, and for myself, a real home. The house empty was a different place from the house occupied.

With so many brothers and sisters, I'd never had many opportunities for privacy. I liked to go into my mother's closet and sit there in the dark for the sheer pleasure of smelling her, at the same time knowing how annoyed she'd be if she knew I'd invaded her privacy. I became a snoop, going through everyone's drawers, looking for clues to how other people lived their lives. I liked to lie on my sister's bed, look out her window, think to myself, *So this is what she sees when she wakes up in the morning.* What was it like to be somebody else? I went into my father's bedroom, dark and cluttered, and saw all the bits of paper, the stray ties, the dirty cups, as marks of how little he was touched by his personal surroundings, how little they, in return, touched him. It all seemed so random, so accidental. In my brother's room I found magazines with pictures of naked women, fascinating me for reasons I couldn't determine. His room seemed the most alien of all. Even when I lay down on his bed and saw what he saw, I knew I wasn't even close.

The long, elliptical mornings of invading other people's

privacy while alone in the house seemed endless, but eventually I'd hear the car drive up to the house and know it was time to leave for the city. Except for Fridays, I looked forward to the drive, counting groundhogs serenely eating grass along the highway, seemingly unaware of the danger a few feet away from them. I pretended I was riding alongside the road with great, graceful swiftness on a large black, gleaming horse, its sensual mane tangling in my face, the rhythm of its hooves a hypnotic lecture on how to arrive someplace entirely different.

Inexorably, Friday, or D-day, as we began calling it, would approach. Wednesday held anxiety at arm's length, but it was there on the edges, and I knew it. Thursday was almost unbearable. Friday morning I woke up early, as always, but I did not want to get out of bed, even to go lie on the floor with my best friends, the dogs, who I imagined understood my suffering and whose wet tongues licking my face weren't random or casual but pointed, intended, full of sympathy.

The second week of chemo was worse in that I knew what to expect. This presented a curious reversal of fear for me, because I already understood that with other types of pain the fear of not knowing about it usually brought about more suffering than the thing itself. This was different. This was dread. It wasn't some unknown black thing hovering and threatening in the shadows; it had already revealed itself to me and, knowing that I knew I couldn't escape, took its time stalking me. This was everything I ever needed to know about Fate.

We went through the whole routine again, the endless

waiting, Dr. Woolf's eternal phone call, his strong hands on my body. I tried not to look at the syringes beside me, but when I looked out the window Dr. Woolf invariably passed in front of my line of vision, casually holding a syringe in the air. When I looked down at the floor, I somehow chanced to look at the exact time and the exact spot where Dr. Woolf would send a brief spurt of fluid out of the syringe to clear the needle of air. A graceful, thin arc of liquid would fall directly onto the tile I was concentrating on. I took it as a sign to cry, which I did, ashamed of myself, unable to meet my mother's eyes as she began telling me not to, to hold it back.

The tourniquet went on, and it began all over again, just like the week before, except that this time when I got home I went straight to bed. I didn't even try to sit up or to eat anything as grotesque as ice cream. I felt that my mother was disappointed with me. I hadn't gone straight to bed last time — why was I doing it this time? She came to my room and sat on the edge of my bed. She looked tired but beautiful, always beautiful to me, her makeup exact and perfect, the redness of her lips, the faint hue of her powder, the distinct, musky smell of her perfume.

"You can't let this get you down, you know. I know it's hard, but you can't get depressed by it. Don't give in to it. You were not so bad last time, so make sure that what you're feeling isn't just in your head."

She sat there a moment longer, staring at me sadly, before asking if there was anything else. When I said no, she stood up and left me alone with the television. My father had rigged up a buzzer to the kitchen, which I could press if I needed anything. For the first few weeks I pressed it every time I threw up, but as time passed and I failed, as I saw it, to not vomit too much, I began leaving the vomit in the bowl, even when it smelled awful, and only buzzed when the large vessel was full. I lay there in my room as if alone in the forest at night, dimly sensing something large breathing close by and feeling the eyes of something unfathomably lurid turning upon me.

My father bought me toys, not because he believed for a second that they would sufficiently compensate me but because it was as close a gesture as he could manage. He didn't really have the stomach for the treatments, and only on the rare days when my mother was ill or busy would he take me in for chemotherapy. His rhythm was entirely different from my mother's. We arrived late, so there was not as much waiting time, though he seemed happy to sit for as long as he could reading the paper. Once my name was called he'd accompany me into the office and exchange greetings with Dr. Woolf, but as soon as I was asked to take off my clothes he'd turn to me and say, "Right then, I'll go get the car." Perhaps in part he was embarrassed to see his daughter half naked, but I knew that he did not want to see me suffer.

He'd jangle the keys at me, just as he did with the dogs, for whom the level of excitement at that familiar sound approached heart attacks. He'd smile and announce, "I'll be right back," adding, "This way you won't have to walk so far when it's over. I'll double-park right outside and come get you."

I watched his back as he left and felt relief, because his

embarrassment and awkwardness caused me as much pain as they did him. There was no blame in those moments, no regrets, no accusations, not even despair. Those things came later, when I learned to scrutinize and judge the past, but at the time his leaving was enabling. Knowing that my father had his own burdens, his own failings, allowed me to continue on through what would otherwise have been unbearable. As an adult, I wonder how he could have left me alone in there, but as a child I knew the answer to this clearly, and knew that as soon as he was out of the room I was, if nothing else, free to respond as *I* chose. My father's nervous whistling of Bobby Sherman's *Julie, Julie, do you love me* faded down the hall as Dr. Woolf turned to me with his tourniquet and I turned to him with my unfettered grief.

My moment of truth with my father was brief, followed mercifully by privacy and a sense of relief. It was harder to maintain a sense of transcendence during the appointments with my mother. She stayed in the room and still, despite my repeated failures, insisted that I not cry. But one summer day — it must have been summer because we were all hot and red-faced — I remember my mother bending beside me. The needle was in my arm, and I was feeling the first hot flushes in my stomach. I could smell her perfume, stronger than usual because of the heat. "Don't cry," she was whispering to me, as if it were a secret we were sharing. Dr. Woolf's voice was resonating over our heads, talking to neither one of us. Perhaps it was something in her voice that day, maybe it was the way everything shone and vibrated with the heat, but for the first time in a long time I lifted my eyes from the still empty basin and looked at her. Her own eyes were filling with water, tears that would never fall but hovered there, only inches from my own.

Suddenly my perception of the world shifted. I wasn't the only person in the world who suffered. I had always heard other children wailing from behind closed doors all along the corridor outside Dr. Woolf's door, so it would be false to say that I found myself hearing them for the first time or more clearly. What happened was more hallucinatory. My sense of space and self lengthened and transformed, extended itself out the door and down the corridor, while at the same time staying present with me, with my mother, who, to my profound discovery, was suffering not just because of, but also for, me.

Moments never repeat themselves exactly. Simply because I understood something important and urgent and graceful there on the examination table, looking at my mother's red-rimmed blue eyes, didn't mean that only seconds later I wasn't back in another moment in which I hated myself for crying, for not being strong enough. The beautifully simple revelation I had with my father in Dr. Woolf's office was followed by his parting, his footfalls dimming down the hall, leaving me alone to contemplate what I had just learned. My mother's very presence forced me to be present, disallowing me to dwell, and the comfort I gained from understanding her pain was both fleeting and insidious. Fleeting because that is the nature of all moments, and insidious because once I had tasted the freedom and transcendence of my epiphany, I wanted only to return to it. I confused that graceful state of mind with the attached solace it brought, so when the next injection came, the next bout of crying, and I *wasn't* able to not suffer I felt I had only myself to blame, felt that I had failed in some unknowable, spiritual way. In my mind I didn't have what it took: I didn't deserve to be comforted.

At night I dreamed that the children I was baby-sitting for had slipped down to the bottom of the pool we were standing by and had drowned. Try as I might, I could never fill my lungs with enough air to reach the bottom, where they lay struggling, the eerie light lapping over them. Afterward their useless corpses rose to the surface. I had to go to their parents, my empty arms outstretched toward them, my clothes soaking wet, and explain what had happened, how I had tried my best, really I had, but still, it wasn't enough.

FIVE

Life on Earth

~

NEXT TO THE GARAGE THERE WAS A SMALL ISLAND
of grass between the sea of driveway asphalt and the front
walk of cement. Smack in the middle, a meager fir tree
splayed its boughs just high enough off the ground for me
to sit in the shade beneath them, the earth dark and sweet
smelling. To the south I was able to survey what amounted
to my version of a grassy plain; to the north a jungle of
thick moss grew up around the mouth of a gutter drainpipe. This was my kingdom. Plastic animals bought at
the local drugstore inhabited it, and together we lived our
urgent lives.

The lion, my favorite, had muscles permanently rippled
into his hard plastic body. He lived in the cave I built for
him out of stones not far from the gutter drainpipe. Every
morning I took him out of the fresh grass bed I'd made
the previous night, and together we surveyed the island,
checking on the other animals safely tucked into their own
domiciles. The aardvark was stashed beneath the tree, the

ibex and giraffe installed on the border of the grassy plain, the zebra roamed between the jungle and the plain, and the snake I relegated to the rocks near the tip of the island. Manufactured by a different company, the snake was slightly incompatible with the other animals in size and coloring, and as a result he never received my most complete care. The animals never came inside the house, never left the island, which to me was the most authentic aspect of their lives.

My mother insisted that I wasn't taking very good care of them when I complained that one of the dogs had chewed on my giraffe or zebra during the night. How could I explain why it was crucial for me, safe inside my bed at night, to think of them out there, living their continuous lives regardless of my presence. I especially loved the nights when the weather became wild, imagining my animals braving the elements, the wind howling and rain beating down. Every morning I had the distinct sense that I was simply opening the door on an ongoing world, constant and sure, that went on into the growing dark even if I was stuck inside, too sick to get out of bed.

When I wasn't on my island, I was riding for the pony express, though sometimes I was a Martian, sent to this planet on a surveillance mission. I was myself only in the briefest of moments, the most passing encounters, a stranger walking brusquely by in the hall. As an alien, I could transform myself anywhere, anytime. Sometimes I was still a human, but one sent here from a future so distant I could in no way comprehend what the everyday things of the present time meant; other times I was an

alien who'd taken on human form and walked imperceptibly among a race that mistook me for one of their own.
Sitting in the car or a waiting room, I'd examine everything around me carefully, objectively. What exactly was
this peculiar ritual of the tollbooth? What was the significance of the different types of footwear? The whole
trick was to forget myself, forget what I really knew, break
all my preconceptions.

The only time I was ever completely myself was on
Fridays. There was no way to escape the pain. Yet with
each successive visit to Dr. Woolf's examining room, my
feelings of shame and guilt for failing not to suffer became
more unbearable. The physical pain seemed almost easy in
comparison. Was this how my body dealt with the on-
slaught, veering the focus away from itself, insisting that
its burden be lessened by having my mind take on more
than its fair share? Whatever the process was, it worked —
worked in the sense that I became adept at handling my
pain, deft at addressing its various complaints and de-
mands for attention.

Afterward I'd lie in bed and concentrate on letting the
tremors run their course, allowing them free access to all of
me so that, like some bear sniffing me out, they'd gradually
grow bored and amble away, leaving me alone and exhausted but still alive. Some pain, like the pain of a needle
or the site of an operation, is specific: it announces itself in
no uncertain terms. Often I tried to balance the pain out
with the rest of my body, a sort of negotiation in which I'd
isolate one section. I'd lie there and list to myself the parts
that didn't hurt, trying to feel them, aware that normally

I'd have no reason to "feel" my body or know it so intimately.

I was becoming aware that I was experiencing my body, and the world, differently from other people. For hours I'd lie in bed either at home or in the hospital and run my finger back and forth along the wall or the bedrails beside me, conversing silently with myself in the third person, rationalizing the situation, setting down the basic premises of my secret philosophy, occasionally even telling myself I was lucky, lucky to have this opportunity to know such things. At times I was desperate and could find no solace anywhere. Nothing seemed to work, and the weight of being trapped in my own body made it difficult to lift even a hand off the sheets. Other times a sort of physical awareness would take hold of me. Each breath was an important exchange with the world around me, each sensation on my skin a tender brush from a reality so beautiful and so mysterious that I would sometimes find myself squealing with the delight of being alive.

Pain centered in my head was the most difficult to deal with. It's one thing to ignore your arm or your stomach, but ignoring your head isn't quite so simple. The radiation treatment was beginning to take its toll, and open sores began appearing all over the insides of my cheeks. The first time I felt them was while eating a bowl of tomato soup. Each mouthful stung, and, since no one had told me that radiation burns were a common side effect, I suspected the soup of being no good. When I thought no one was looking, I carried my bowl from the living room, where I was eating in front of the television, into the bathroom, where I overturned it into the toilet. The soup sunk in scarlet, silty swirls to the bottom of the white porcelain, and I let it lie there for a few moments before flushing it away. I didn't want to say anything to my mother because I was afraid she'd see this as yet another of my ploys to not eat. I was losing weight rapidly, and everyone seemed to be shoving food in my face, food I had little interest in. Eating had become a monumental effort, and I couldn't explain to my mother or the nurses that simply finishing one boiled egg was tantamount to an act of heroism.

Now there was a new item on the already long list of why it was hard to eat: not only did I have trouble chewing and swallowing, not only was my stomach in turmoil half the time, but now it actually *hurt* to put food in my mouth. It got worse. As the radiation treatment went on, I could eat only the blandest of foods. Any sort of fruit was out of the question: drinking orange juice felt like I was rinsing my mouth out with battery acid. Anything salty or even vaguely spicy, such as ketchup, ignited my tongue and the raw, tender skin of my cheeks. I lived almost exclusively on oatmeal, disgusting protein drinks that practically had to be forced down my throat, and endless dozens of junk-food chocolate cream rolls, my mother's welcome bribe for the protein drinks. I loved eating entire boxes of these disgustingly sweet and fatty things slowly and with embellished delight in front of Susie and Sarah, who were eternally on some new diet.

After every six weeks, I was admitted to the hospital, to my beloved Babies 10, for a five-day course of intensive che-

motherapy. I actually looked forward to these times in the
hospital. The doctors set up the IV and administered the
yellow fluid slowly and continuously, which didn't make
me feel as intensely ill as the weekly injections of a concentrated dose. And if I did feel ill, I simply threw up in my
basin and lay back in my white bed, secure in knowing
that no one cared too much if I threw up or not, cried or
not: I felt free and sovereign. I was considered a "regular
customer" on the ward. I knew all of the nurses, knew the
routines and the jargon, and often found myself explaining things to the rookie doctors who rotated on and off the
ward. With no school responsibilities to speak of, no family tensions to deal with, I considered going into the hospital something just short of a vacation.

Even now, hospitals elicit intense nostalgia in me, the
vague longing that attaches itself to almost any version of
the past, as if it is context, not content, that really counts.
A feeling rises up in me, and though I know I was often in
pain, I remember myself as being happy in the hospital,
lying in the heavily starched sheets, hearing the sounds
and movements of other people just outside the door.

At home it was different. Those long quiet mornings in
the house still gave me pleasure, but as soon as the silence was
broken, as soon as anyone entered the front door, tension
and shame accompanied them. Unable to locate my unhappiness within the difficult and complex family relationships
we all shared, I thought that it all originated with me, that I
was somehow at fault. If I couldn't overcome my growing
depression, I deserved it, and how unfair of me to inflict it
upon everyone else, upon my mother especially.

I was willing to try anything to get out of the weekly chemo shots. The only way to do this was to be too sick to withstand it. Holding the thermometer up to the light bulb's heat and other elementary-school tricks were ancient history. I had to be *really* sick, had to have a measurable increase in my white blood cell count, indicating an infection.

My first experiment in making myself ill came about innocently. It was a Thursday in early winter, and everyone was asleep except my father, who was working late again. Icy rain was falling all over the state. News reports warned people not to drive if they could avoid it. The temperature was hovering just at thirty-two degrees. The local television station showed a map of New York with cotton-ball clouds floating over it, clouds weeping blue raindrops mixed with white circles of hail. The whole picture looked like the thought balloons over cartoon characters' heads, as if New York State itself was *considering* icy rain, thinking it over.

I lay in bed thinking about my island, and suddenly I was overcome with a desire to go outside and see how my animals were faring in the storm. I thought of the real cows I'd seen from the car, standing staunchly in their fields, shivering, the black part of their hides gleaming wetly, a faint steam rising from them. I got out of bed and pulled down my long flannel nightgown, which had bunched up around my waist in bed. Without bothering to put on shoes, I walked toward the garage door and let myself out as quietly as possible, trying not to waken the dogs. I felt the chill run up my legs.

My animals were fine, just where I'd left them. I was disappointed that the rain only shellacked their bodies instead of being absorbed into them in dark, shiny streaks, as real skin and hair would allow. Standing there, only a few feet from the door, I began to shiver. That's when it hit me that if I stayed outside I was going to catch cold. I was going to get sick, perhaps even sick enough to raise my white blood cell count. It seemed like the perfect plan. Walking into the dark back yard, I found a spot where I knew that no one looking from inside the house would be able to see me, and lay down on the cold wet grass. I tried looking up at the black, chalky sky, but the rain kept splashing into my eyes, forcing me to close them. How long would I have to stay out here? What would I do with the evidence of my wet nightgown? If I hung it near the heater, would it dry before my mother saw it in the morning? The cold began to get painful. My teeth chattered. If I couldn't stay out here long enough, if the discomfort of the cold drove me inside before I had a chance to get really ill, would that mean I was a failure even in this?

My nightgown soaked through, making it almost transparent. I could see my tiny nipples, pink and hard, and below them, my sharp hips sticking up. I lay there until I couldn't stand it anymore, until my fingers were stiff and red and starting to swell. Once inside again, I pulled off my nightgown and hung it over a chair. If my mother found it, I would tell her I'd thrown up on it and washed it myself in the sink. It was sensual and delicious to be back in my warm bed, the sheets absorbing the water from my naked skin. I fell asleep almost instantly, a rarity for me.

But the next morning I felt fine. I woke up and saw the wrinkled nightgown still on the chair and remembered what had happened. I breathed in deep, expecting to hear soft rales in my lungs, but there was nothing, not the slightest hint of congestion. Sitting up, I tried to gauge how I felt. Did I have a fever? Was my throat sore, did I feel weak at all? No. I felt perfectly fine. I didn't even feel tired. In fact, I felt better than I had all week, which seemed like the cruelest joke, seeing that it was Friday, and in only twelve hours I would be right back in this same bed, throwing up.

I sought out different ways of getting sick. I experimented with drinking dishwashing liquid, but all that did was make me *feel* ill without actually *being* ill. I was too scared to try any other poisons I could find under the sink, having met two boys in the hospital whose lips, tongues, and throats had been burned away from drinking substances found beneath the sink. Roy, the one boy I was friends with, had a feeding tube in his nose, which he swung about like an elephant's trunk. Charlie, the other mouthless boy, was younger and had a mean look in his eye; whenever I was admitted to the ward I scanned the chart list for his name, hoping he wasn't there.

My pet project was inhaling water. Once, while nauseous, I'd inhaled some of my own vomit, and my lungs had reacted instantly with a case of pneumonia. Unfortunately for me, the pneumonia came right before Christmas, at the very end of a cycle of shots, when they were planning to stop anyway. If I could somehow get a small amount of fluid into my lungs, I figured I'd be set. I filled the bathtub and on the count of three submerged my head. Breathe, I'd tell myself, *breathe*. I saw it as a battle of my own will. I saw it as a test of *forcing* myself. I'd lie there until I ran out of breath, reemerge for air, then sink back under again, firmly telling myself that this time I was going to do it. When I finally found it in myself to open my mouth under water after countless attempts, my body would automatically heave itself up, sputtering water. For a moment my mouth and maybe even my throat filled with water, but the violent coughing I couldn't suppress prevented the water from reaching my lungs. The water in the bathtub sloshed around me and splashed over the sides, and the white towels, soaked from mopping up the water on the floor, hung like flags of surrender over the tub.

Most drastically, I experimented with scratching my arms with rusty nails I found lying on the street. A case of tetanus — the lockjaw everyone thought I'd had in the very beginning — still seemed preferable to chemo. I re-member sitting on the stone steps in our back yard one afternoon, the summer sun glaring down. I was listening to the screams of the neighborhood children I hardly ever played with anymore and trying to scratch myself with the top of a dirty tin can. Again something held me back; while I could raise a good welt, I never scratched forcefully enough to break the skin or draw blood. Something always held me back, and for the longest time I thought it was cowardice.

Letters from strangers all across the country started arriv-ing in the mail. Somehow my name had found its way

onto a Catholic prayer list. The letters, on colored station-
ery bordered with flowers, cats, intricate motifs, were usually short, written in rounded hands. All of them assured
me that Jesus loved me, and if I loved him he would take
on his share of the burden. One woman sent me a picture
taken from her kitchen window, a snowy back yard with a
bird feeder covered with sparrows. "When I'm sad," she
told me, "I look at my birds, and they make me happy."
Letter after letter confessed similar thoughts, advised me
to think happy things, think of kittens, of foods I like to
eat. My family got a kick out of reading these letters. With
our bitter, cynical air we mocked them out loud, laughing
at their naiveté, their unbounded simplicity. Every letter
promised a prayer said in my name.

I laughed along with my brothers and sisters, but part of
me longed for the world of those letters, just as I longed for
the world I watched on television, on *Father Knows Best*
and *The Brady Bunch*. I fantasized about these shows,
imagining what would happen if one of their children
got cancer. Everything would be talked about, everything
dealt with. No one would ever lose his temper. No one
would go unnoticed.

Along with the letters came pamphlets, Christian publications mostly geared toward children. They told stories
of mysterious strangers who appeared on the doorsteps of
troubled families, strangers with a special shine to them, a
kind look and a light in their eyes. A quality of calmness
and fairness infused the difficult tasks the stranger performed, whether mediating an argument between parents
or helping an invalid. He glowed with love and peace and

understanding. The aura was as palpable as a physical feature, and everyone who met him could not help but notice it. After a few days he would leave the family, having impressed upon them how they too could be happy and peaceful if only they let God into their lives.

In the secrecy of my room, I decided I wanted this light, this peace, this glow. But the scenarios always ended the same way, with the stranger leaving and the troubled family left alone to ponder and resolve to change. I always wanted to turn the page, to know how or what the troubled family could actually *do* in order to believe. After all, I was sold, I *wanted* to have Jesus help me out and make me good and strong and pure, all of the things I was sure I wasn't — but exactly *how* was I supposed to do this?

Sooner or later we're all driven to this point. In secrecy, away from my family and our shared scorn over the cards and their simplistic sentiments, I sat down in my bedroom on the blue carpet and asked, "God, if you exist, prove it to me."

What was I expecting? A voice, a verbal affirmation? A physical one? I looked down at the carpet, half expecting it to change color. A sudden light, maybe? I looked up into the air above my head for it. I knew I only half expected an answer. Was my partial belief preventing God from speaking to me? Didn't I have to *fully* believe, or did all this simply mean that there *was* no answer? I hugged my knees close into my chest and rocked back and forth on my heels. I couldn't bear to think I was wrong, that somehow everything I was going through didn't actually have meaning.

I stretched my arm out in front of me and flexed it, opened and closed my fingers. I resolved to Believe, even in the face of this lack of response. Was it possible to prove my worthiness by repeatedly asking the question, even in the brunt of this painful silence? In the same way I was sure I could prove my love, and lovability, to my mother by showing her I could "take it," I considered the idea that what God wanted from me was to keep trying and trying and trying, no matter how difficult it was. My goal, and my intended reward, was to understand.

Life became more complicated at home when my father lost his job in the news department at ABC. The loss of his job meant the loss of his medical coverage. Luckily my mother's job was able to take up part of my coverage, but we were still in a bind. Family life became more tense. Days were filled with phone calls and letters and endless forms. Nights were filled with even more arguments about money. Under my father's plan, the hospital pharmacy had sent the drugs used in my treatment up to the clinic. Now we had to pick up and pay for the drugs ourselves. To my extreme horror, this meant we had to store them in the refrigerator at home. Every time I opened its door, there they were, a row of short glass vials lined up in the butter rack. The cold light glinting off them made my stomach lurch.

For some inexplicable reason, the new coverage, so inadequate in so many ways, paid for an ambulance to transport me to the hospital each day. The notion thrilled me. But the day the ambulance actually pulled up in front of our house I felt self-conscious and awkward as I walked down the lawn. A group of neighbors had come out to see what was happening and stood there in a circle, watching. "I'm not really that sick," I wanted to tell them. "This is just a big joke, get it?" Though I knew I'd lost weight and was a bit pale, I never considered myself all that sick. I thought of myself as separate from them because of what I'd gone through, but it didn't occur to me until then that people might actually *pity* me. The idea appalled me.

Horrified as I was that people might feel sorry for me, I also knew that I possessed a certain power. After all, people noticed me. Wherever I went, even just to the store with my mother, I was never overlooked. I could count on some sort of attention, and I discovered that people were embarrassed when I caught them looking at me. I stared right back at these strangers with my big blue eyes, which appeared even bigger now that I'd lost weight and now that, without bone to shape it, the right side of my face was starting to sink in. They always looked away quickly, trying to pretend they hadn't been staring.

If this type of attention wasn't always comfortable for me, it nonetheless further defined me. Most people struggle all their lives to avoid fading unnoticed into the crowd, but this was never my concern. I was special. Being different was my cross to bear, but being aware of it was my compensation. When I was younger, before I'd gotten sick, I'd wanted to be special, to be different. Did this then make me the creator of my own situation?

The ambulance rides continued for only a few weeks. Then my father got a new job at CBS and I was again covered by his medical insurance, meaning no ambulance and no more storing the drugs in the refrigerator. I was relieved on both counts. My mother and I once more took up our daily drives to the hospital. The whole way there I stared out the window and as before imagined myself on a horse, galloping along the strip of grass beside the road, jumping the irrigation ditches and road signs.

SIX

Door Number Two

⌐

EARLY ON IN THE TREATMENT MY HAIR BEGAN TO fall out. Although I had been warned, I was taken by surprise the first day I reached up to sweep my hair back and found a handful of long blond hair in my hand. I guess I'd never believed this really would happen. I was sitting in the car with my mother when I first noticed it, and I started to cry. At a loss to say anything that would truly comfort me or stop my hair from falling out, my mother reminded me that I had known this would happen, that I shouldn't get so upset — as if foreknowledge of an event could somehow buffer you from its reverberations. Feeling, again, that I had failed simply by being upset made me cry harder.

I'd never thought much about my hair. I had been complimented on it, but such remarks had never particularly interested me. More often than not, my hair seemed like a bother to me, something that got in the way when I wrestled or climbed trees. But now? When I undressed at night, I heard the static of my sweater as I pulled it over my head, then saw the long strands on the collar waving in the breeze of its electricity. I'd sit up in bed in the morning and look down at the tangles of hair on my pillow. As water ran out of the bath, I had to sit on the edge of the tub and reach over several times to free up the drain. Once an aggressive, careless brusher, I now patted at my head with a comb very carefully and very gently.

Involved as I was with the physical process of losing my hair, I somehow ignored the change in my appearance. I knew I was going bald, I knew I was pale and painfully thin, I knew I had a big scar of my face. In short, I was different-looking, and I knew my face had an effect on other people that I could sometimes use to my advantage. But I was still keeping myself ignorant of the details of my appearance, of the specific logic of it. My intuition must have known it was better this way.

In the same way that I understood the extent of my illness while not actually admitting I was ill, I spent a very long time not acknowledging that I was going bald, even as I swept my own hair off the dog's black coat after a particularly vigorous hug. I was too young, only ten, almost eleven, to be any Samson. Sex appeal belonged to toothpaste commercials, while sex itself was still a mysterious thing, clues to which could be found in the pages of my brother's magazines. Though the pictures were mysteriously compelling, I mostly found them slightly repulsive, and I regarded sex, whatever it was, as something I'd surely never take part in. I looked at myself in the mirror with a preoccupied preadolescent view, which is to say that I looked at myself but didn't judge myself. When the first taunts and teases were thrown at me, usually by some strange kids in the supermarket parking lot, more often than not I was able to come back with an insult far more sarcastic and biting than their own rather unimaginative Baldy or Dog Girl. I understood that their comments were meant to impress each other more than harm me. I possessed a strong sense of myself — and I lived vividly in my world of hospitals and animals and fantasy. I had no sense of myself in relation to the "normal" people I walked by every day. I was naturally adept at protecting myself from the hurt of their insults and felt a vague superiority to them, for the moment, anyway.

Sometimes when I was in the hospital, days or even a week would pass before I was well enough to get up and wash my hair. I hated the way it got oily and lanky and bunched up in tangles behind my head from lying on it so long. That first morning when I could get up and wash it was always a great relief. But finally one morning, when I asked my mother to help me wash it, she looked at me sorrowfully and suggested, in a kind voice, "Maybe it's time to cut it." And that's what we did. She borrowed a pair of scissors from the nurse's desk, and while I sat in a chair she snipped off what remained of my hair, my white, white scalp shining through. We discovered for the first time that I had a large birthmark above my left ear.

The next morning my mother came in with a hat, a small white sailor's hat, which I put on and almost never took off for the next two and a half years, even during the periods when my hair was growing back in. Sometimes it grew several inches and was perfectly presentable as hair, but I knew it was only going to fall out again, and I refused to be seen in public without my hat. My hat. It became part of me, an inseparable element of who I thought I was.

My hat was my barrier between me, and what I was vaguely becoming aware of as ugly about me, and the world. It hid me, hid my secret, though badly, and when people made fun of me or stared at me I assumed it was only because they could guess what was beneath my hat. It didn't occur to me that the whole picture, even with the hat, was ugly; as long as I had it on, I felt safe. Once, on television, I saw someone lose his hat in the wind and I immediately panicked for him, for his sudden exposure. It was a visceral reaction.

As the teasing continued, both from strangers and from the very boys whom I'd once regarded as friends, I began to suspect that something was wrong. I identified the problem as my baldness, as this *thing* that wasn't really me but some digression from me, some outside force beyond my control. I assumed that once the problem was solved, once my hair grew back in, I would be complete again, whole, and all of this would be over, like a bad dream. I still saw everything as fixable.

During this time my mother was working in the Occupational Therapy Department of a Hasidic nursing home, and most of my mother's coworkers were Hasidim. Hasidic custom dictates that once a woman is married she must cover her hair. This used to be done with kerchiefs, but now most of the women wore wigs. I imagine they grew tired of their wigs the same way other women grow tired of their clothes, because there seemed to be a surplus of discarded wigs in the community. As my mother's friends became aware of my predicament, they generously began to donate these hand-me-down hairpieces. My mother didn't know how to refuse them, and the first time she came home with a wig we all had a good time in the kitchen playing with it, trying it on ourselves first and then on the cats. When I put it on, I looked as ridiculous as my brothers and sisters, not to mention the cats, so it was all a big safe joke.

But more wigs kept coming home with my mother. Sometimes it seemed she had a new one every day, and the house began to fill up with them. Each emerged as more atrocious than the last; it was impossible to take any of them seriously. When her friends at the nursing home asked how the wigs had worked out, my mother politely but truthfully told them that none of them fit me properly. One of my mother's closest coworkers offered the services of her wig maker, who would measure my head and make one "just the way I wanted it, just like my real hair." Not wanting to appear ungrateful, I, coached by my mother, thanked this woman and agreed to go for a fitting, with the unspoken understanding between my mother and me that I did not really want a wig.

We drove to New City, a nearby town with a large Jewish population, and found the store in a small cluster of shops. I'd never been to a "parlor" before, and somehow I'd envisioned a fancy salon filled with glamorous women. But the room was harshly lit, with long overhead fluorescent bulbs, and instead of Warren Beatty, whom I'd seen in *Shampoo*, we were greeted by a small, old man who was bald himself. He affectionately beckoned me to sit in a chair facing a mirror framed with roughly carved pink and gold flowers. A large, dusty rubber plant with leaves as big as my head filled one corner of the room.

"So, the little girl wants a wig, eh?"

He smiled at me in the mirror. I shriveled inside, mortified beyond any realm I'd previously thought possible. He turned to my mother, and they began speaking, his hand resting on my bird-thin shoulder. I kept watching him in the mirror, not because I was fascinated by him, but because I didn't want to look at myself. I knew the moment was coming when he'd ask me to take off my hat. I knew there was nothing I could do about it except pretend I didn't care, and when he turned back to me and the moment finally came, I took off the hat as nonchalantly as possible and placed it in my lap. I kept my gaze directed at him in the mirror while he took out a measuring tape and ran lines over the various angles of my head. I liked this part. My hair was growing in at that point — it was about half an inch long — and his dry hand stroked the babylike fineness of it with a tenderness that made the back of my neck go all goose flesh.

After the measuring, he went to the back room to get different samples. Knowing I'd had long blond hair, he brought back wigs of varying lengths and shades of blond, ranging from bright yellow to almost brown. He placed each one in turn on my head and discussed with my mother which types were closest to my "natural" state. He explained that all of the wigs were made of human hair, which made me envision a bizarre blend of the Christmas story "The Gift of the Magi," in which a woman sells her hair for the sake of love, and the Holocaust, where I knew they'd shaved the heads and kept the hair of people about to die horrible deaths.

Now it was unavoidable; I had to look at myself in the mirror. As each wig was put on and adjusted, both the man and my mother would ask me what I thought, but all I could manage was a sullen nod or shake of the head. Looking at myself in these wigs, with their dull, however human, hair, horrified me, and each time the man commented on "how natural" it looked I could only see him, and eventually myself, as that much more alien.

How long was this going to go on? How many wigs were there in the world, anyway? Though inside I was growing more and more petulant, I made halfhearted efforts to look happy, and when the last wig was finally tried on, I actually smiled when the old man asked how I liked it. I hated it. At last the issue of cost came up, which in my mind signaled the end of this charade. I knew my mother would never want to pay for something as ludicrous as a wig, and besides, hadn't we more or less agreed we weren't really going to get one? The man quoted an astounding sum, far higher than we could have even joked about. I sat in the chair, my feet swinging, ready to leave, and watched the reflections of my mother and this man talking in the mirror. To my great amazement, I saw a look on my mother's face that seemed to say she was actually considering ordering one of these overpriced, custom-made patches of hair. Could she be serious? I looked on in amazement, and when we finally left the store it was with a promise that she would think it over and call him tomorrow.

Once we were in the car, I thought she would look at me and we'd both laugh, share our private joke, but instead she turned and addressed me seriously. "Well, do you want one? It's a lot of money, but if you want one, I'll buy it for you."

What had happened? I thought we'd only gone to be polite to her friend. Wasn't it obvious how hideous those wigs were, how alarming? I didn't know how to reply. Back at home she called up her friend to tell her what had happened, and I heard her say, "It was the first time in a long time I've seen her smile. She hasn't smiled in so long."

So that was it. Normally I was intuitive and could guess what was going on behind people's words and actions, but if my own mother could be so wrong about me, how could I know I wasn't mistaken in my own interpretations?

To keep the situation from getting too far out of hand, I went to my mother and told her outright that I didn't want a wig, that I thought they were ugly. She looked relieved because of the expense, but as she looked at me and smiled I thought again of what she'd said on the phone. I smiled at her, sick in my heart at this newly discovered chasm opening up between me and the rest of the world, as if there weren't enough chasms already. But out of my compulsion to continually seek the truth I questioned her about her conversation with her friend, which I saw as a betrayal of me. I insisted I was okay, happy even, that the wig was a big joke. She smiled back at me even more broadly, relieved to see my old self, and for that moment I was happy, content that I could at least give her that.

I kept on wearing my hat. But I couldn't shake the image of my face staring back at me with that ludicrous, grotesque halo of a wig. Did they actually mean it when they said, "Now doesn't that look nice?" I felt quite certain that I looked awful in those wigs, yet why did my belief not seem to match up with everyone else's? Were they lying to me? Perhaps they didn't want to hurt my feelings. It was dawning on me that I might look much worse than I had supposed.

One morning I went into the bathroom and shut the door, though I was alone in the house. I turned on the lights and very carefully, very seriously, assessed my face in the mirror. I was bald, but I knew that already. I also knew I had buck teeth, something I was vaguely ashamed of but hadn't given too much thought to until this moment. My teeth were ugly. And, I noticed, they were made worse by the fact that my chin seemed so small. How had it gotten that way? I didn't remember it being so small before. I rooted around in the cabinets and came up with a hand mirror and, with a bit of angling, looked for the first time at my right profile. I knew to expect a scar, but how had my face sunk in like that? I didn't understand. Was it possible I'd looked this way for a while and was only just noticing it, or was this change very recent? More than the ugliness I felt, I was suddenly appalled at the notion that I'd been walking around unaware of something that was apparent to everyone else. A profound sense of shame consumed me.

I put the mirror away, shut off the lights, went back into the living room, and lay in the sunlight with the cats. They didn't care how I looked. I made a silent vow to love them valiantly, truly, with an intensity that would prove I was capable, worthy of . . . I wasn't sure what, but something wonderful, something noble, something spectacular. I repeated the same vow to the dogs.

My father worked odd hours, leaving late in the morning and not arriving home until long after dark. He'd cook his own dinner and eat it standing up near the sink while staring contemplatively out of the viewless and dark kitchen window. Some nights I'd get out of bed and go visit him there. He'd hear me pad into the room and stare at me, his face surprised for only a moment before it transformed into genuine pleasure at seeing me. "Lucinda Mag," he'd announce, as if he were only just then naming me, and I'd sit down on a chair, pulling my nightgown over my knees, stretching the material tight. He'd sit down at the table with me and eat in silence while I watched, both of us perfectly content.

One night when I walked in he was wearing one of the wigs. They littered the house by then, and we'd grown careless with them. The cats slept on them, the dogs played tug of war, and they were still good for a few laughs when visitors put them on.

My father was standing over the stove, stirring a panful of something sizzling. "Lucinda Mag," he announced, grinning, inviting me to tell him how silly he looked. I didn't. I simply sat down as always and watched him finish cooking and eating his solitary meal until finally I couldn't stand it anymore.

"Daddy, take it off."

"Take what off?"

"The wig."

"What wig? I'm not wearing a wig."

"Daddy."

"I have no idea what you're talking about."

It went on like this. I knew he was joking, and I knew he had no idea how much I *really* wanted him to take the wig off. I gave up. Freeing my knees from my nightgown, I walked over to him, pushed the long hair aside, and kissed him good night.

I was still experimenting, unsuccessfully, with making myself ill. Pneumonia remained my pet plan, though I was still unable to inhale the water. Summer had arrived, so there was no hope of catching cold outside, but I'd seen enough trapped-in-the-desert movies to hope for heat stroke. I didn't have a clue what heat stroke was, but the word *stroke* made me envision some sort of tender caress. I did know that it involved seeing mirages. I wasn't allowed to go into the sun because of the extra radiation, so any exposure that might give me a tan was out.

I wrapped myself in a blanket and went to lie in my private spot in the back yard. I lay there and felt the ants crawl up on my skin. Although I liked ants and bugs in general, I occasionally tortured them, then felt guilty and sinful afterward. I'd vow not to, but I always did it again. I was finally cured after reading a German fairy tale that described a horrible little girl who liked to pull the wings off flies. When she died and went to purgatory, she was doomed to have all the flightless little lives she'd ruined crawl all over her and get in her mouth and eyes. I stopped my tortures not out of morality but from a combination of self-preservation and disgust.

Sunlight came through the blanket in pinhole streams. Birds and chainsaws sang and wailed in the background. It was sweltering. I sat up and pulled the blanket cowl-like around my head and stared into the distance. Sweat rolled down the side of my rib cage, a rib cage so skinny I could feel the drops momentarily rest above the ridge of each bone. I stared into the distance. I was looking for my mirage. In the movies they saw either water holes or beautiful women, sometimes both. My eyes scanned the back yard: nothing. My T-shirt now was drenched with sweat. Even the backs of my hands were sweating, and my scalp, which itched against the blanket. I realized this wasn't going to work. Lifting myself up with great effort, I walked back into the air-conditioned house, the wave of cold hitting my face like a bucket of water when I opened the door.

The one time I actually got out of having chemotherapy, I wasn't even feeling particularly ill. But when the blood test showed a high white blood cell count, I was overjoyed. Deciding I should be put into isolation for a bit, a porter came down to the clinic to collect me in a wheelchair. I loved riding in wheelchairs, and I waved gaily to Dr. Woolf as I was chauffeured past him.

"Better not look too happy," my mother advised me. Immediately I went into my waif mode, a style I'd been perfecting for some time. Since becoming slowly aware of my odd appearance, I'd decided to use it for all it was worth to have an effect on people, to matter somehow.

Isolation wasn't such a thrill after all. Because my admission was unexpected, I hadn't come prepared with books or toys, and, horror of horrors, the room had no television. I wasn't permitted to have any of the ward's shabby toys brought in because of germs, and there was no view, because the only window was blocked by a broken air conditioner. I kept opening the door to stick my head out, but someone always yelled at me to shut it, to stay inside and get back into bed. I felt perfectly fit. How could I really be ill? Lying face down on my bed, I felt my hipbones jut down into the overstarched sheets. Sleep was a long way off. I saved myself only by pretending I was a prisoner put "in the hole," which I'd read about in a book about a group of men in prison, a book I knew I wasn't supposed to read because in it the men had sex with the prison's mascot, a donkey. I lay there and pretended I'd been framed.

That week was the exception, though. Most weeks Friday was still D-day. The chemotherapy became my entire life for two and a half years. To fill the time as I waited to see Dr. Woolf, I'd go to the public bathroom down the hall. I loved the feeling of my small body traveling in the same direction as all those large bodies in suits and white jackets striding effortlessly past me, street shoes clicking on the tile.

It was an old bathroom with only two stalls. Each stall door was wooden and closed on the inside with a silvery metal latch. There was no graffiti anywhere in the bathroom except on these latches. Someone, certainly the same person, had scratched onto each rectangular piece of metal a message. Sitting on the toilet in the first stall you could read *God Is Near,* and on the second, *Be Here Now.* I always pictured the person who wrote these messages sitting on the same porcelain as myself, bending forward, one arm raised up and resting against the warping wood of the door, a nail file in the other hand. I sensed that it had been done a long time ago, before my time. What was wrong with them? I wondered. Why were they here? I never asked myself what might have happened to them.

Still spending my private moments trying to engage God in conversation, alternately attempting to barter him into answering my questions and silently trying to listen to the answer, these bathroom communications seemed important to me.

Each Friday I'd plod down to this bathroom, killing time before the inevitable, and I'd pause for a moment before the two doors, trying to decide which message I wanted to read. *God Is Near.* Well, okay, how near? Did this mean he was near in the way someone is near when they're coming toward you, moving closer and closer, not yet here but expected sooner or later? Or did it mean he was near but not showing his face, present but unseeable, someone breathing quietly in a closet? *Be Here Now.* I didn't want to be here now. My wanting was inconsequential. I *was* here now, whether I liked it or not. But something about this saying attracted me, either despite or because of its seeming simplicity, and two out of three times I went for door number two.

Some weeks I stared at it dumbly, thinking only of what was happening back in the waiting room with my mother, how many more rows of knitting she'd finished. Some weeks I thought of the impending injection, or I simply continued with my fantasy life: the pony express rider seeks relief in the town's saloon, the alien ponders the wonders of waste disposal. Some weeks, especially when it was hot, I thought of nothing and only listened to my urine hiss into the water below my legs as I leaned forward, pressing the coolness of the inscribed metal against my forehead, and wept.

SEVEN

Masks

⏤

HAVING MISSED MOST OF FOURTH GRADE AND ALL
but a week or so of fifth grade, I finally started to reappear
at school sometime in sixth grade during my periodic
"vacations" from chemotherapy. I'd mysteriously show up
for a week or two weeks or sometimes even three or four,
then disappear again for a couple of months.

Most of the sixth-grade class consisted of children I'd
grown up with. They were, for the most part, genuinely
curious about what had happened to me. They treated me
respectfully, if somewhat distantly, though there was a
clique of boys who always called me names: "Hey, girl,
take off that monster mask — oops, she's not wearing a
mask!" This was the height of hilarity in sixth grade, and
the boys, for they were always and only boys, practically
fell to the ground, besotted with their own wit. Much to
their bewilderment and to the shock of my teachers, I
retorted by calling out to them, "You stupid dildos."

Derek used to say that word all the time, and I thought

it a wonderful insult, though I didn't have a clue as to what a dildo was. After being reprimanded enough times for wielding this powerful insult, I finally asked my brother what it meant: an artificial penis, he informed me. I gave up using the word. I'd known children in the hospital with artificial limbs, and I'd known children with urinary tract problems.

The school year progressed slowly. I felt as if I had been in the sixth grade for years, yet it was only October. Halloween was approaching. Coming from Ireland, we had never thought of it as a big holiday, though Sarah and I usually went out trick-or-treating. For the last couple of years I had been too sick to go out, but this year Halloween fell on a day when I felt quite fine. My mother was the one who came up with the Eskimo idea. I put on a winter coat, made a fish out of paper, which I hung on the end of a stick, and wrapped my face up in a scarf. My hair was growing in, and I loved the way the top of the hood rubbed against it. By this time my hat had become part of me; I took it off only at home. Sometimes kids would make fun of me, run past me, knock my hat off, and call me Baldy. I hated this, but I assumed that one day my hair would grow in, and on that day the teasing would end.

We walked around the neighborhood with our pillow-case sacks, running into other groups of kids and comparing notes: the house three doors down gave whole candy bars, while the house next to that gave only cheap mints. I felt wonderful. It was only as the night wore on and the moon came out and the older kids, the big kids, went on their rounds that I began to realize why I felt so good. No one could see me clearly. No one could see my face.

For the end of October it was a very warm night and I was sweating in my parka, but I didn't care. I felt such freedom: I waltzed up to people effortlessly and boldly, I asked questions and made comments the rest of my troupe were afraid to make. I didn't understand their fear. I hadn't realized just how meek I'd become, how self-conscious I was about my face until now that it was obscured. My sister and her friends never had to worry about their appearance, or so it seemed to me, so why didn't they always feel as bold and as happy as I felt that night?

Our sacks filled up, and eventually it was time to go home. We gleefully poured out our candy on the floor and traded off: because chewing had become difficult, I gave Sarah everything that was too hard for me, while she unselfishly gave me everything soft. I took off my Eskimo parka and went down to my room without my hat. Normally I didn't feel that I had to wear my hat around my family, and I never wore it when I was alone in my room. Yet once I was alone with all my candy, still hot from running around on that unseasonably warm night, I felt compelled to put my hat back on. I didn't know what was wrong. I ate sugar until I was ready to burst, trying hard to ignore everything except what was directly in from of me, what I could touch and taste, the chocolate melting brown beneath my fingernails, the candy so sweet it made my throat hurt.

*   *   *

The following spring, on one of the first warm days, I was playing with an old friend, Teresa, in her neat and ordered back yard when she asked, completely out of the blue, if I was dying. She looked at me casually, as if she'd just asked what I was doing later that day. "The other kids say that you're slowly dying, that you're 'wasting away.'" I looked at her in shock. Dying? Why on earth would anyone think I was dying? "No," I replied, in the tone of voice I'd have used if she'd asked me whether I was the pope, "I'm not dying."

When I got home I planned to ask my mother why Teresa would say such a thing. But just as I was coming through the front door, she was entering from the garage, her arms laden with shopping bags. She took a bright red shirt out of a bag and held it up against my chest. It smelled new and a price tag scratched my neck.

"Turtlenecks are very hard to find in short sleeves, so I bought you several."

I was still a tomboy at heart and cared little about what I wore, just so long as it wasn't a dress. But turtlenecks — why on earth would I want to wear turtlenecks in the spring? I didn't ask this out loud, but my mother must have known what I was thinking. She looked me straight in the eye: "If you wear something that comes up around your neck, it makes the scar less visible."

Genuinely bewildered, I took the bright-colored pile of shirts down to my room. Wouldn't I look even more stupid wearing a turtleneck in the summer? Would they really hide my "scar"? I hadn't taken a good long, objective look at myself since the wig fitting, but that seemed so long ago, almost two years. I remembered feeling upset by it, but I conveniently didn't remember what I'd seen in that mirror, and I hadn't allowed myself a close scrutiny since.

I donned my short-sleeved turtlenecks and finished out the few short months of elementary school. I played with my friend Jan at her wonderful home with its several acres of meadow and, most magnificent of all, a small lake. There was a rowboat we weren't allowed to take out by ourselves, but we did anyway. Rowing it to the far shore, a mere eighth of a mile away, we'd "land" and pretend we'd just discovered a new country. With notebooks in hand, we logged our discoveries, overturning stones and giving false Latin names to the newts and various pieces of slime we found under them.

Jan had as complex a relationship to her stuffed and plastic animals as I had to mine, and when I slept over we'd compare our intricate worlds. Sometimes, though not too frequently, Jan wanted to talk about boys, and I'd sit on my sleeping bag with my knees tucked up under my nightgown, listening patiently. I never had much to offer, though I had just developed my very first crush. It was on Omar Sharif.

Late one night I'd stayed up and watched *Dr. Zhivago* on television with my father. Curled up beside him, with my head against his big stomach, I listened to my father's heart, his breathing, and attentively watched the images of a remote world, a world as beautiful as it was deadly and cold. I thought I would have managed very well there, imagined that I would have remained true to my passions had I lived through the Russian Revolution. I, too, would have trudged across all that tundra, letting the ice sheet over me and crackle on my eyebrows. For weeks I pictured the ruined estate where Zhivago wrote his sonnets, aware that the true splendor of the house was inextricably bound to the fact that it was ruined. I didn't understand why this should be so, and I didn't understand why reimagining this scene gave me such a deep sense of fulfillment, nor why this fulfillment was mingled with such a sad sense of longing, nor why this longing only added to the beauty of everything else.

Elementary-school graduation day approached. I remembered being in second grade and looking out on a group of sixth-graders preparing for graduation. It had seemed like an unimaginable length of time before I'd get there. But now I was out there mingling in the courtyard, remembering the day when I laid my head down on the desk and announced to the teacher, "I'll never make it." I could even see the classroom window I had gazed out of. So much had happened in four years. I felt so old, and I felt proud of being so old. During the ceremony I was shocked when the vice-principal started speaking about *me*, about how I should receive special attention for my "bravery." I could feel the heat rising in me as he spoke, my face turning red. Here I was, the center of attention, receiving the praise and appreciation I'd been fantasizing about for so many years, and all I could feel was intense, searing embarrassment. I was called up onto the platform. I know everyone was applauding, but I felt it more than heard it.

In a daze I accepted the gift Mr. Schultz was presenting me with, a copy of *The Prophet.* I could barely thank him.

Later, alone in my room, I opened the book at random. The verse I read was about love, about how to accept the love of another with dignity. I shut the book after only a page. I wanted nothing to do with the world of love; I thought wanting love was a weakness to be overcome. And besides, I thought to myself, the world of love wanted nothing to do with me.

The summer passed, and junior high school loomed. Jan, Teresa, and Sarah were all very excited at the prospect of being "grownups," of attending different classes, of having their own locker. Their excitement was contagious, and the night before the first day of school, I proudly marked my assorted notebooks for my different subjects and secretly scuffed my new shoes to make them look old.

Everyone must have been nervous, but I was sure I was the only one who felt true apprehension. I found myself sidling through the halls I'd been looking forward to, trying to pretend that I didn't notice the other kids, almost all of them strangers from adjoining towns, staring at me. Having seen plenty of teen movies with their promise of intrigue and drama, I had been looking forward to going to the lunchroom. As it happened, I sat down next to a table full of boys.

They pointed openly and laughed, calling out loudly enough for me to hear, "*What* on earth is *that?*" "*That* is the ugliest girl I have *ever* seen." I knew in my heart that their comments had nothing to do with me, that it was all about them appearing tough and cool to their friends. But these boys were older than the ones in grade school, and for the very first time I realized they were passing judgment on my suitability, or lack of it, as a girlfriend. "I bet David wants to go kiss her, don't you, David?" "Yeah, right, then I'll go kiss your mother's asshole." "How'll you know which is which?"

My initial tactic was to pretend I didn't hear them, but this only seemed to spur them on. In the hallways, where I suffered similar attacks of teasing from random attackers, I simply looked down at the floor and walked more quickly, but in the lunchroom I was a sitting duck. The same group took to seeking me out and purposely sitting near me day after day, even when I tried to camouflage myself by sitting in the middle of a group. They grew bolder, and I could hear them plotting to send someone to sit across the table from me. I'd look up from my food and there would be a boy slouching awkwardly in a red plastic chair, innocently asking me my name. Then he'd ask me how I got to be so ugly. At this the group would burst into laughter, and my inquisitor would saunter back, victorious.

After two weeks I broke down and went to my guidance counselor to complain. I thought he would offer to reprimand them, but instead he asked if I'd like to come and eat in the privacy of his office. Surprised, I said yes, and that's what I did for the rest of the year whenever I was attending school. Every day I'd wait for him, the other guidance counselors, and the secretaries to go on their own lunch break. Then I'd walk through the empty outer office and sit down in his private office, closing the door behind me.

As I ate the food in my brown paper bag, which crinkled loudly in the silence, I'd look at the drawings his own young children had made. They were taped to the wall near his desk, simplistic drawings in which the sky was a blue line near the top and the grass a green line near the bottom and people were as big as houses. I felt safe and secure in that office, but I also felt lonely, and for the very first time I definitively identified the source of my unhappiness as being ugly. A few weeks later I left school to reenter chemotherapy, and for the very first time I was almost glad to go back to it.

My inner life became ever more macabre. Vietnam was still within recent memory, and pictures of the horrors of Cambodia loomed on every TV screen and in every newspaper. I told myself again and again how good I had it in comparison, what a wonder it was to have food and clothes and a home and no one torturing me. I told myself what fools those boys at school were, what stupid, unaware lives they led. How could they assume their own lives were so important? Didn't they know they could lose everything at any moment, that you couldn't take anything good or worthwhile for granted, because pain and cruelty could and would arrive sooner or later? I bombed and starved and persecuted my own suffering right out of existence.

I had the capacity of imagination to momentarily escape my own pain, and I had the elegance of imagination to teach myself something true regarding the world around me, but I didn't yet have the clarity of imagination to grant myself the complicated and necessary right to suffer. I treated despair in terms of hierarchy: if there was a more important pain in the world, it meant my own was negated. I thought I simply had to accept the fact that I was ugly, and that to feel despair about it was simply wrong.

Halloween came round again, and even though I was feeling a bit woozy from an injection I'd had a few days before, I begged my mother to let me go out. I put on a plastic witch mask and went out with Teresa. I walked down the streets suddenly bold and free: no one could see my face. I peered through the oval eye slits and did not see one person staring back at me, ready to make fun of my face. I breathed in the condensing, plastic-tainted air behind the mask and thought that I was breathing in normalcy, that this freedom and ease were what the world consisted of, that other people felt it all the time. How could they not? How could they not feel the joy of walking down the street without the threat of being made fun of? Assuming this was how other people felt all the time, I again named my own face as the thing that kept me apart, as the tangible element of what was wrong with my life and with me.

At home, when I took the mask off, I felt both sad and relieved. Sad because I had felt like a pauper walking for a few brief hours in the clothes of a prince and because I had liked it so much. Relieved because I felt no connection with that kind of happiness: I didn't deserve it and thus I shouldn't want it. It was easier to slip back into my depression and blame my face for everything.

* * *

Hannah was a cleaning woman in Dr. Woolf's office. She was quite old, or at least seemed old to me, and she wore a cardigan summer and winter. Her domain, when she wasn't polishing the hallway floors or disinfecting the metal furniture, was an oblong room off the main doctors' hallway, just a few doors down from Dr. Woolf's. I appreciated this room because it was painted pale blue, so unlike the sickly green that dominated the rest of the place. During the last year of chemotherapy I'd grown considerably weaker, and sometimes walking the few blocks to the parking lot after the injection seemed an insurmountable task. On particularly bad days my mother would leave me in Hannah's care while she went to fetch the car. Hannah would sit me down in a chair next to a small table with a kettle and some cups on it, her own small island where she took breaks.

The routine never varied. She knelt in front of me and asked, "How do you feel?" I could hear her slip rubbing between her stockings and dress. Looking her straight in the eye I'd confidentially report, "My nose hurts."

It was always such a relief to be able to admit this to her. I later learned why the chemo affected my sinuses, but as far as I could tell, Hannah was the only one who believed this comic complaint. She'd nod sympathetically and offer me a cup of tea, and I would politely refuse. Then we would sit and stare at each other, waiting for my mother to return. I knew that beyond a cup of tea, there was nothing she could offer me. But her gaze soothed me. Normally I despised the looks of others, but with Hannah I felt a vague sense of camaraderie, imagining that both our little lives were made miserable by these unknowing, cloddish doctors. To her I was probably just one of the many sick children who streamed in and out of the place, but in my mind I'd found a silent link with someone whose life was as difficult as I found my own. As ill as I felt, I always liked sitting there with her, imagining our parallel lives clicking quietly along like two trains beside each other, with similar routes but different destinations.

When I played with Jan or Teresa, my friends from that time now indelibly labeled *Before,* they treated me the same way they always had, though perhaps with an air of delicacy that seemed uncomfortable and unnatural for all of us. They asked me questions about the physical effects of my treatment — how much it hurt, why I was so skinny, when my hair would grow back. I loved to answer with vigor and embellishment. A third of my answers were shaped by the braggart's love of a good tale, another third by my instinctive knowledge that they'd never understand what it was really like, and a third by my own unawareness of what it was like a great deal of the time. I witnessed my life unfolding like someone who has awkwardly stumbled in after the movie has started. I sensed that something important had been revealed in the opening sequence, some essential knowledge everyone else was privy to that was being kept from me.

I could converse with well-intentioned neighbors, go the usual round of polite questions about my health, though I was highly aware of how different these conversations were from the ones with my friends on Ward 10, my friends from *After.* People who weren't ill or involved in the daily flow of hospital life had their own ideas of what it was like to be ill. It seemed impossible to tell them how it really was, and I didn't particularly want to do so. I preferred to have strangers on the street imagine me as sickly, confident that as soon as I was back on Ward 10 my friends and I would redefine for each other what it was like to be sick.

I felt as if my illness were a blanket the world had thrown over me; all that could be seen from the outside was an indistinguishable lump. And somehow I transformed that blanket into a tent, beneath which I almost happily set up camp. I had no sense of how my life was *supposed* to be, only of how it was. Not that this meant I was actually happy, not in any normal definition of the word. Though I depended on my apocalyptic thoughts to keep my situation in perspective, they did imbue me with a rather depressed aura. "For God's sake, stop looking so morbid all the time" became a familiar phrase in my house. Whenever anyone else was present I felt incapable of being anything other than a depressed lump. It was only when I was alone that my ability to relish life surfaced.

Each week, with the first glimmer of returning strength after the days of vomiting, I discovered that, for me, joy could be measured in negative terms: of what I *didn't* have, which was pain and weakness. My greatest happiness wasn't acquired through effort but was something I already had, deep and sonorous inside of me, found through a process of removing the walls of pain around it. I knew the walls were inside of me, and I saw that most people, never having experienced deep physical discomfort on a regular basis, didn't, couldn't, know this.

I viewed other people both critically and sympathetically. Why couldn't they just stop complaining so much,
just let go and see how good they actually had it? Everyone
seemed to be waiting for something to happen that would
allow them to move forward, waiting for some shadowy
future moment to begin their lives in earnest. Everybody,
from my mother to the characters I read about in books
(who were as actual and important as real people to me),
was always looking at someone else's life and envying it,
wishing to occupy it. I wanted them to stop, to see how
much they had already, how they had their health and
their strength. I imagined how my life would be if I had
half their fortune. Then I would catch myself, guilty of
exactly the thing I was accusing others of. As clear-headed
as I was, sometimes I felt that the only reason for this
clarity was to see how hypocritically I lived my own life.

Once, during a week of intensive chemotherapy toward
the end of the two and a half years, I was sent to another
ward, as 10 was already full when I checked in. My roommate was a girl who'd been run over by an iceboat; the
blades had cut her intestines in two, and she'd had to have
them sewn back together. She got a lot of attention, lots of
calls from concerned relatives and school friends, and I
was both a little jealous of her and a little contemptuous
because she was taking her accident a bit too seriously for
my taste. After all, she'd lived, hadn't she? She'd had one
operation and they might do another one the next week,
but after that it would all be over, so what was the big fuss
about?

It was late at night, always a bad time in the hospital, but especially on this ward, which I'd been on before and which was notoriously understaffed. Often there was only one nurse and a handful of aides to take care of everyone. This was particularly bad news if you had an IV. They were still using butterfly needles instead of the flexible catheter-type needles they have today. The needle was inserted into the back of your hand and simply taped down to the skin. The chances of it puncturing the vein were high, and I'd learned to keep that hand absolutely still, even in my sleep. Worse, however, the limited staff often neglected to refill the IV bottles regularly and they would dry up in the night, causing the needle to clot with blood. Many nights I had to be woken three or four times in order to be restuck with a new butterfly. My veins were so tired that often it took three, four, even five sticks before the doctor, who was never happy to be woken for the menial task of setting up an IV, could get the fluid to flow properly. I learned not only to sleep without moving, for fear of hitting the needle out of place, but also to sleep in two-hour shifts so that I could wake up and check the bottle's fluid level myself.

This particular night I woke up on that strange ward and looked at the bottle in the blocks of light coming in through the city window. To my relief it was still half full. The light coming in passed through the clear solution and threw a marbled reflection down on the floor. I had to go to the bathroom. I tried to assess if I could walk the few feet unaided and decided I couldn't. Pressing the call button for a nurse, I sighed, realizing it wasn't a buzzer system, as they had on other floors, but simply a bulb that would light up over my door in the hallway. Chances were good that no one would see it for some time. I waited. I waited and waited and even tried calling out, but my voice couldn't carry that far. My roommate slept soundly, still heavily sedated from her operation that morning. I saw her open mouth, her fat cheeks, her whole face turned upward toward the ceiling as her thick, curly hair fell to the side.

She'd spent all of yesterday's dinnertime telling me about her parents' divorce, about how her father came to get her each weekend and always took her to do something. This weekend they had gone ice sailing. She spoke of it in a passive yet unhappy voice. While she was in surgery I listened to her mother fight with her father, accusing him of causing the accident. He yelled back at her and, in my mind, won. They all seemed very impressed with the complications of their lives, with their divorce and their fights and their daughter, who commanded the divided attention of her parents. Who would ever understand how jealous I was?

I kept waiting to see if a nurse would come. How much time passed I don't know, but I had to make a decision: get up and walk or pee in the bed, as I'd done once before in a similar situation. For a brief time during my father's unemployment I'd gone on Medicaid and had been sent to a completely different part of the hospital, to a gigantic open ward that was disturbingly understaffed. I called and called for a nurse or an aide, but finally I couldn't stand it any longer and, with great relief, let go and peed right there in the bed. I had to lie in it until it was cold and had spread through all of the sheets before an aide finally, almost comically, walked in with a bedpan. She looked at me disapprovingly and said she'd send someone to change my sheets. Ten minutes later a woman showed up and looked at me in surprise. She asked me how old I was, and I told her eleven. She shook her head and said that when she heard someone had peed in the bed, she thought it must have been a baby.

I wasn't going to go through that embarrassment again. All I had to do was be strong, I told myself, and I could make it to the bathroom. Sitting up wasn't hard at all. Slipping down to the floor was fine as long as I did it slowly. Grabbing hold of my IV pole, which was on the wrong side of the bed, adding extra length to the journey, I began the seven or eight feet to the bathroom. I passed the foot of my bed. Even at this hour, traffic was still audible outside. My roommate breathed heavily, almost snoring but not quite, while my IV swayed and clinked against the metal pole as I pushed it along. I neared the foot of her bed and had almost passed it when I understood I would never make it. I was exhausted. I had to sit down, but the one chair in the room was even farther away than the bathroom or my bed. Tiredness and a creeping ache so overwhelmed me that I forgot I even had to go to the bathroom. Could I make it back to my bed? It was too far. Suddenly afraid I was going to faint, I crouched down to the floor, aware that I was adopting the pose of the crouched skeletal figures in the countless famine pictures I studied so hard in news magazines. *I'm okay,* I told myself, *I'm okay.*

I thought that if I could just rest like that for long enough, I'd regain the strength to make it back to bed. The five feet might as well have been five miles. My knees began to ache, and afraid that I might fall even from this crouch position and dislodge the IV, I gingerly lay down on the floor. My hipbones and elbows hurt against the hard floor. If I lay here long enough, would someone come by and see me? After all, my call light was still on. What would they think, seeing me lying here? Maybe they'd feel sorry for me, maybe they'd sweep me up in their arms, place me back in bed and lay a comforting hand across my forehead, whisper something sweet and consoling in my ear.

Until that moment I had believed in the drama of my life, the dramatic possibilities my tragedy called up. But now the floor was cold. The floor was just so cold. I didn't want to lie there anymore, and even though it would take a Herculean effort to ease myself back up, I didn't want to wait anymore for someone to come rescue me. I suddenly had a glimmer of what the person had meant when he scratched that message into the bathroom door eleven floors below: Be Here Now. I felt a bottomless sense of peace, of stillness. I decided it was simply a matter of will, that if I really concentrated I could make it back. And I did. It took a long time and I don't remember anything once I was back in bed. I must have fallen asleep immediately, only to be woken from a deep sleep a little while later by an aide, answering my call light at last.

*   *   *

"Do you realize this is the last six weeks?" my mother asked late one Thursday afternoon while starting to prepare dinner.

"What?"

"The last set of shots. Only six more, and then all this will be over. What a relief. You must be overjoyed."

I was shocked. Over? It was almost over? I looked at her, speechless. "Thank God for that," I said, using a phrase she employed all the time.

I went down to my room and lay on my bed, utterly confused. Why wasn't I overjoyed? I was almost thirteen years old. I'd been doing this since I was ten; I barely remembered what life had been like before. No more shots, no more Dr. Woolf, no more throwing up. I was afraid, and I was afraid that I was afraid. Why wasn't I happy, the way I was supposed to be? What was wrong with me? I didn't want it to continue, did I? No, I knew I didn't, but life after chemo seemed unimaginable. Bewilderment filled the room. As hard as it was to admit this to myself, I was afraid of it ending, of everything changing. I wouldn't be special anymore; no one would love me. Without the arena of chemotherapy in which to prove myself, how would anyone know I was worthy of love? But how could I ever want it to go on? I lay there turning these things over and over in my mind, more perplexed than I'd ever been in my life.

Counting off the days became an obsession. Thirty-eight more days until the last shot. Thirty-two more days. Fifteen more days. Three days and eighteen hours. Forty-eight hours and nineteen minutes. Three hours. Sixteen minutes. Now. I walked into Dr. Woolf's office, and it didn't seem in any way special or different. It was a bit gray outside, a bit chilly, but not exactly cold. Dr. Woolf was all business as usual, on the phone, talking in five different directions at once. For only the second time I looked at the syringes in the basin. There were two of them, and one was filled with a bright red solution the color of Kool Aid. I watched him attach the needles, watched him walk carelessly around the room with them, still on the phone but to someone different now. Then he put the phone down and put the tourniquet on and rubbed my arm with a cotton ball, the smell of rubbing alcohol filling the air. As usual, it took a few stabs to find a vein, but the third one worked.

The hot flashes came, followed by the familiar nausea, and I painfully retched up nothing but the single Thorazine pill I'd been given an hour before. It was meant to help the vomiting, but every week I only threw it up, and there it was again, half dissolved, pinging into the basin. Slowly I realized that I wasn't crying. These last few months I had hardly cried at all: it wasn't that I actually cried less but that I controlled it more. Not crying had become the goal of my visits to the chemotherapy clinic. But now I felt absolutely nothing. My mother was praising me for being so good. I looked at her and at the beautiful window behind her. Robotically, I looked back to my arm, to Dr. Woolf's huge hands changing syringes. Nothing. I felt only a void. Even the usual pain floated around me. It seemed to belong more to the room than to me, and even then awkwardly, like a clumsy piece of furniture.

Then it was over. My mother and Dr. Woolf were talking. I couldn't hear them, though they were right next to me. I was looking at the ceiling. It was peeling, and there was a water stain just off to the right. Funny, I thought to myself, all that time looking around and never noticing the ceiling. Had I never looked at it, or had I looked at it dozens of times, only now really *seeing* it? My mother finished speaking with Dr. Woolf and turned toward me; then she, too, before helping me off the table, wordlessly looked up for a moment, following my gaze.

She went off to get the car, and I was ushered into Hannah's room. "How do you feel?" she asked. I began to cry. Just a little bit at first, but soon I was sobbing and my whole body was shaking. I tried to stop, but it was out of control, and I gave myself over to it. Hannah bent over and put an arm on my shoulder for a second, only for a second, then withdrew it and straightened up. She stood there for a few moments holding her hands together over her stomach, then, without asking, busied herself making me the cup of tea she'd been offering me for years. Through my sobs, which were getting loud now, I heard the water rattle and hiss inside the electric kettle. My lungs were already filled with sorrow, and though I didn't think it was possible, I cried even harder.

A few minutes later, Hannah handed me the tea in a mug with a picture of the Statue of Liberty on it. Holding the hot mug in my hands, I cried just as hard, though conscious now that I mustn't spill the tea. My head was pounding. Slowly the crying began to stop. I felt so tired all of a sudden, but quietly tired, in a restful way, not the usual exhaustion. By the time my mother returned, I had stopped, not because of any effort on my part but because the crying had run its course. We said good-bye to Hannah and walked out. No one on the streets, bending their heads down into the cold wind, seemed to notice or care that this day was different from others.

EIGHT

Truth and Beauty

~

ONE DAY, WHEN I HAD A FULL THREE OR FOUR INCHES of hair, I was leaving the house with Susie. At the last minute I turned and ran back up the stairs, calling out, "Just a minute while I get my hat."

"You don't need it anymore, Lucy, your hair is fine, come on already," she called back to me, frustrated that we were going to be late.

I stopped in the middle of the stairs and, genuinely surprised, considered what she had said. Running my fingers through my hair, I had to admit she was more or less right. It wasn't nearly as long as it used to be, but I wasn't bald. I went out with her into the world, bareheaded for the first time in years. A warm and gusty breeze parted my hair and stroked it like a caress. We went to the store, and people gave me second looks as they always did, but not one person called me Baldy.

The next day I went to school bareheaded, and no one mentioned it. Had I been wrong in thinking that I needed to hide behind my hat, had it all been a mistake on my part? Except people still looked at me. Though I had given up eating in the lunchroom, there were plenty of relentless daily attacks of teasing in the hallways. Girls never teased me, but out of the corner of my eye I could see them staring at me, and when I turned toward them, they glanced away quickly, trying to pretend they were concentrating on something else. Outside of school I'd catch adults staring at me all the time. I played games with them in stores, positioning myself just so and pretending I was absorbed in examining some piece of merchandise, only to turn my head quickly and trap them as they averted their embarrassed stares. Groups of boys were what I most feared, and I gladly ducked into an empty doorway if I saw a group coming my way that looked like trouble. It was easy to spot potential offenders: they walked with a certain swagger, a certain sway.

My relief — tinged with regret — at leaving the familiar and well-ordered world of the hospital didn't last very long. The radiation had been very hard on my teeth, the lower ones especially, and saving them would require a lot of specialized work. Only a few short months after I naively thought I'd said good-bye to Columbia Presbyterian Hospital forever, we had to again start the routine of driving in once or twice a week for what turned out to be two years of dental work. The dental clinic was in a completely different part of the hospital, though we still walked through the courtyard that Dr. Woolf's office looked out onto. The hospital laundry was somewhere nearby, and the smell of it, which I associated with the walk to Dr. Woolf's, never failed to make me a little bit queasy.

There was, however, the benefit of getting out of school. By now I hated school with a vengeance and continually told lies about my health in order to stay away. Anything just to not have to face those boys each day. Luckily, my mother was fairly compliant; looking back, I wonder that I was allowed to pass into the eighth grade at all with my attendance record.

The various procedures, including at least a dozen root canals, kept me in pain most of the time. Codeine was prescribed. We kept the refillable prescription bottle in a kitchen cabinet, and within a short while I was taking pills almost constantly, even when I wasn't in pain. I looked forward to the pleasant, sleepy feeling they offered. No matter how bad I felt about the world, about my position in it, I felt safe and secure and even rather happy thirty or forty minutes after I'd downed a couple of pills. As the months wore on and that pleasant effect became harder to achieve, as each pill seemed to touch the pain less, I started taking more and more pills. I was aware that I was taking more than I should, up to four times the regular dose, and I would alternately ask my mother and then my father to refill the prescription in order to keep my high consumption less conspicuous. They both noticed that the pills seemed to be disappearing quickly, but they assumed my brothers were pilfering them. All of this came to an abrupt end one day when my mother caught me shaking out no less than six times the prescribed number of pills into my palm. From then on I had to make do with aspirin.

My inability to open my mouth very wide caused a lot of problems whenever anyone wanted to work on my back teeth, and it was decided that I should be admitted to the hospital and have a whole slew of work done all at once under general anesthesia. This idea was fine by me. Not only did it offer even more days off from school, but the thought of surgery seemed far more appealing than sitting wide awake in that dreadful dentist's chair.

This was my fifth operation, a number that seemed high at the time. On the morning of the operation, an aide woke me early and tossed a surgical gown and a small bottle of Betadine onto my bed. I was to wash my whole body and my hair with this iodine solution, put on the gown, and then wait in bed until the nurses came with the pre-op injection needles. This was the worst part of all. The waiting felt endless, crowded with an unspoken dialogue inside my head concerning the nature of pain.

It gave me pleasure to think that the boys who teased me openly at school and the adults who stared at me covertly elsewhere would never be able to stand this pain, that they would crumple. My whole body was tense and my stomach upside down, but I was convinced that because I did not admit these things, did not display them for others to see, it meant I had a chance at *really* being brave, not just pretending. Every time I heard footfalls coming down the hall, fear's physical rush swelled inside me, and as the footfalls passed my room, a physical sense of relief came over me. These false alarms, however, only heightened my fear, knowing that sooner or later the approaching steps would really be for me.

When the moment came, a student nurse gripped my hand tightly, almost too tightly, squeezing the blood from my fingers, as a regular nurse injected my thighs with the premed. Paradoxically, the moment after the injection, which made my thighs ache and sting, came as a relief; every tension fell and floated prettily away like leaves from an autumn tree. As the minutes passed, the sweet and strange comfort of the medication lifted me up and floated me around the room, and when the orderly finally arrived and asked me to slide over onto the stretcher, I felt as if I were watching someone else shyly try to hold the short gown down over her legs as she awkwardly wiggled along the rough sheets.

When the operation was over I remember throwing up some swallowed blood and feeling terribly weak, though joyously relieved it was all over. In post-op the specially trained nurses checked on me every ten minutes. I was too groggy to sense what was going on, but I relished the aura of attention, the cool hands on my warm arms, the way my name distantly sounded in their soft, I-won't-let-anything-bad-happen-to-you voices, the notion that I was somehow special, that I mattered. But afterward, back in my room, I dozed and waked for hours, each time more panicked than before at being all alone. I'd make up some excuse to ring for a nurse, just to have someone enter the room. I began to wish that the operation weren't over, that I was still asleep on the stretcher with a crowd of people hovering near me.

Later, as I underwent more and more operations, even when I was home in my own bed, upset about how much I hated my face, I could put myself to sleep by imagining myself lying on a stretcher. I could almost hear the movements of strangers in comfortingly familiar uniforms all around me, the distant beeps that were really heartbeats, the mechanical shushes of respirators, which meant someone, somewhere near, was breathing.

It wasn't without a certain amount of shame that I took this kind of emotional comfort from surgery: after all, it was a bad thing to have an operation, wasn't it? Was there something wrong with me that I should find such comfort in being taken care of so? Did it mean I *liked* having operations and thus that I deserved them?

At school the taunts were becoming only harder to take. Somehow I had reasoned that if a bad thing happened often enough it would get easier. It worked with pain, so why wasn't it working with teasing? Every time I was teased, which usually happened several times a day, it seemed incrementally more painful. I was good at not listening, at pretending I hadn't heard, but I could sense myself changing, becoming more fearful. Before I'd been an outgoing person, and in the right circumstances I still was, but now meeting new people was laced with dread. Except for the one time I went to my guidance counselor to complain, I discussed this with no one. Besides, I reasoned, what could I do about it? I was ugly, so people were going to make fun of me: I thought it was their right to do so simply because I *was* so ugly, so I'd just better get used to it. But I couldn't. No matter how much I braced myself, the words stung every time they were thrown at me. It didn't seem to matter that I was doing everything I could to know the truth, to own the fact that I was ugly, to make sure I was prepared for it, to be told nothing I didn't already know.

One afternoon I went to the hospital for some outpatient surgery. A tooth in the back of my mouth had to be pulled, and I was knocked out for about ten minutes. Afterward I waited in recovery for my mother to take me home. When she came in, she pulled the blood-soaked gauze out of my mouth and gasped. In the course of the surgery two of my lower front teeth had been partially knocked out, leaving two very ugly stumps. Apparently no one had been planning to tell us about this complication, and it was only by chance that my mother discovered it while we were still there. Justifiably, she exploded in anger. The surgeon's response was predictably patronizing, and a full-fledged battle ensued as I sat there feeling a bit woozy and slightly bewildered, still pleasantly lost in the fading buzz of the anesthetic.

Once home, my mother, still fuming, turned to me and said, "You don't have to go to school tomorrow if you don't want. I understand that you might not feel very good about the way your teeth look." We looked straight at each other. Something had just happened, but I wasn't sure what. All I'd ever wanted was to be left alone and allowed to stay at home. I had spent a great deal of energy trying to convince her that I had to stay at home because of some counterfeit physical ailment, and suddenly it wasn't what I wanted at all.

She stood over me in the living room, the cats howling for their dinner because we'd returned home so late from the hospital, and offered me, what, compassion? As I think of it now, I'm certain her offer to let me stay home was an attempt to understand what she must have known instinctively. But it was too late. I'd already given up that fight. I understood my mother's offer only as barbed verification of what I believed to be the indisputable truth: I was too ugly to go to school. I pretty much stopped going to the seventh grade, but I was moved along with everybody else to the eighth. My grades were mediocre, and my passing surely had to do more with ineptitude on the school's part than with academic accomplishment on mine.

I relished that summer as no other. My friend Jan and I took our infatuation with horses to ridiculous proportions. We spent all of our play time pretending we were horses, galloping around her yard, jumping over whatever obstacle we could set up. Whoever got around better was given a homemade blue ribbon, and afterward we would kneel on her lawn and dare each other to graze, the curiously familiar and sour flavor of grass filling our mouths and turning our front teeth green.

Jan's parents were paying for her to take riding lessons that summer, and I was filled with envy. We couldn't afford them. Sometimes she'd invite me to go with her and I would, though I hated the superior tone she took with me then. I went because the very presence of horses overwhelmed me, filled my whole body with a sensation so physical and complete that I'd be transported during those hours. I did nothing but fear the passing of each moment as I sat by the fence watching Jan ride, because I knew that eventually we'd have to go home and all I would have left was the wonderful, peaty smell on my palms to remind me of the horses. Jan started boasting that her parents were going to buy her a horse, that they'd build a stable for it in the empty field by the lake, and that, maybe, just maybe, she'd let me help her take care of it. We spent long afternoons thinking up names for the horse, though according to my taste, her ideas were sentimental, unoriginal choices such as Beauty and Black.

Jan never got her horse, but that June, shortly after my fourteenth birthday, I got my job as stable hand at Diamond D. It was the perfect environment for me. Most of the other hands were girls who were a couple of years older than me, and there were two boys, Sean and Stephen. The girls were nice enough to me and eventually became my friends, though I never felt completely at ease with them. We came from different worlds. They were raucous and wild, and I loved them for this. Epithets the likes of which I'd never heard even from my own wild brothers flew from everyone's lips, and there was a glorious delight in getting as muddy and dirty as possible. When I came home at the end of the day my mother always made me undress in the garage. I was proud of the mud all over me and the tired ache from trying to hoist bales of hay, however ineffectually. As the summer wore on I got tanned and gained weight and grew physically stronger every day.

I loved how basic were the needs of the animals, how they had to be fed and watered even if you were tired or hot or late. There was a primacy to it, a simplicity I recognized from coping with the pain of my treatments, a shedding of all extraneous grievances to reveal a purely physical core, a meaning that did not extend beyond the confines of one's body. When feeding time was near, pandemonium broke out among the horses, filling the barn with neighing and kicking and squealing. And as soon as our work of dragging buckets and hauling hay was over, peace descended. It was a quiet filled with chewing sounds and soft snorts and a sense of rest that felt ancient and good. Sometimes late at night, when I couldn't sleep, I would call the barn, knowing no one was there, and imagine the sound of the phone echoing in the horse-filled barn.

I kept my new world, with its physical pleasures and new social experiences, completely hidden from my family, who did not seem particularly interested anyway, though they were glad I'd found something "healthy" to do with my time. School was coming around again, and I actually looked forward to returning: horse fever is common among junior high school girls, and I thought my new job at the stable might improve my status at school. Everyone at the barn was preparing to return to school as well, including Jeanne, who was boy crazy and had a crush on Sean.

The day before school began, some six of us girls were sitting on top of the hay pile. Jeanne stood on top, pointing to each person and asking, "If Sean asked you out, would you go with him?" The girls were mixed in ages and in physical development, Jeanne being the oldest at sixteen. Alison and I, at fourteen, were the youngest. Alison looked fourteen, but I, my body still reeling from the effects of all the chemotherapy, looked about ten. Puberty was still a year away. Jeanne seemed to be asking everyone systematically, but she wasn't actually thinking of asking me, was she? Sean would never ask me out; it was a completely ridiculous question, and the thought that we all might have to acknowledge this fact together seemed worse than anything else in the world.

Finally, Jeanne turned to me and, only because she didn't know how to politely leave me out, asked the question. I hesitated, not sure how to respond, but then Chris came to my aid and answered for me. "Why would Sean want to go out with her?" "Well, I'm just asking," Jeanne replied. I shifted uncomfortably on the hay, glad Chris had spoken for me. This was the moment when I knew definitively that I would never have a boyfriend, that no one would ever be interested in me in that way. I suppose I had learned this already from the boys at school, but never had I actually formed the inner sentence, expressed it in real terms to myself.

Because I was never going to have love (this realization, too painful to linger over, I embraced swiftly and finally), I cast myself in the role of Hero of Love. Instead of proving my worth on the chemotherapy table, I would become a hero through my understanding of the real beauty that existed in the world. I decided that it was my very ugliness that allowed me access to this other beauty. My face may have closed the door on love and beauty in their fleeting states, but didn't my face also open me up to perceptions I might otherwise be blind to? At the end of each day, as I lay in the bathtub, I looked at my undeveloped child's body. I considered the desire to have it develop into a woman's body a weakness, a straying from my chosen path of truth. And as I lay in bed at night, I considered my powers, my heightened sense of self-awareness, feeling not as if I had chosen this path, but that it had been chosen for me.

Beauty had nothing to do with the ephemeral world of boys, of this I felt sure. This was driven home to me when junior high school started again and I watched my sister and her friends begin their own puberty. They put on blue eye shadow, blow-dried their hair, and spent interminable hours at the local mall. My own notions of what made a woman beautiful were more classically oriented: if I could look like anyone in the world it would be either Marlene Dietrich or Botticelli's Venus. I definitely did *not* aspire to look like Farrah Fawcett, of this much I was sure. I looked at girls in my class, with their perfect faces, and wondered why on earth they ruined them with so much makeup, such stupid hair. If *I* had a face like that, I told myself — then harshly reprimanded myself for any stirrings of desire. My face was my face, and it was stupid to wish it any other way.

At school the gang of boys from last year appeared to have dispersed, and I was free to eat in the lunchroom again. But a new group had formed, and they tracked me down every day between fourth and fifth periods as I went from gym to English class, which were at opposite ends of the school. By the time I reached the staircase near my English classroom, nearly everyone else was already there, leaving me to climb the stairs alone. Alone, that is, until that group of six boys discovered they could find me in this stairwell each day at the same time and took to waiting for me. Their teasing was the most hurtful of all because it wasn't even directed at me but at a boy named Jerry.

"Hey, look, it's Jerry's girlfriend. Hey, Jerry, go on, ask your girlfriend out." I heard Jerry meekly protest, but I knew that he was as much at their mercy as I was, and I knew that to have me called his girlfriend was just about the most malicious insult the other boys could level at him. I even felt sorry for Jerry, though I never saw him, for I refused to lift my gaze from the floor. What morons, I thought to myself, what misguided morons. Martin Luther King, one of my heroes, had said, "I will not allow my oppressors to dictate to me the means of my resistance." That seemed like a far truer thing, a far deeper thing. I wanted to hate them, but instead I tried to forgive them. I thought that if I could do this, the pain they caused would be extinguished. Though I had genuine glimpses of what charity and transcendence meant, I was shooting for nothing less than sainthood; often, after my daily meeting with them, I only ended up hating myself instead.

The horses remained my one real source of relief. When I was in their presence, nothing else mattered. Animals were both the lives I took care of and the lives who took care of me. Horses neither disapproved nor approved of what I looked like. All that counted was how I treated them, how my actions weighted themselves in the world. I loved to stand next to them with no other humans in sight and rest my head against their warm flanks, trace the whorls in their hide with the fingers of one hand while the other hand rested on the soft skin of their bellies. All the while, I'd listen to the patient sounds of their stomachs and smell the sweet air from their lungs as attentively as if I were being sent information from another world.

In the middle of the school year, several months before my fifteenth birthday, I went to see Dr. Conley, the surgeon who had removed my jaw, to discuss plans for reconstructing it. I had known all along that something was going to be done to "fix" my face, but up until this point I don't think I had really believed it.

Without the threat of chemo or dental work, being in a doctor's office seemed so simple and easy. As Dr. Conley examined me, he held my head in his hands, touching my face as no else had in years. It was only then that I realized how guarded I had become about my face; simply relaxing and allowing him to touch me there was akin to surrender, the closest I ever got to experiencing trust. After the examination, he sat down and spoke to me in the tone of someone speaking to a child, which served to both instantly destroy and strangely build the trust in him I had felt only moments before.

He explained that the biggest obstacle to reconstruction would come from all the radiation treatments I'd undergone. Irradiated tissue tends not to take grafts too well and presents a higher rate of reabsorption; even if the graft wasn't actually rejected, it might simply be "taken back" by my body and shrink down to nothing. He proposed a technique that required the use of "pedestals," which would require several operations. In the first operation, two parallel incisions would be made in my stomach. The strip of skin between these incisions would be lifted up and rolled into a sort of tube with both ends still attached to my stomach, resembling a kind of handle: this was the pedestal. The two incisions would be sewn together down its side, like a seam. Six weeks later, one end of the handle would be cut from my stomach and attached to my wrist, so that my hand would be sewn to my stomach for six weeks. Then the end of the tube that was still attached to my stomach would be severed and sewn to my face, so that now my hand would be attached to my face. Six weeks after that, my hand would be cut loose and the pedestal, or flap, as they called it, would be nestled completely into the gap created by my missing jaw. This would be only the first pedestal: the whole process would take several, plus additional operations to carve everything into a recognizable shape, over a period of about ten years altogether. Ten years! I was horrified. I would be twenty-five years old in ten years: ancient. Did I have to devote the next ten years of my life to one surgery after another? Ten years — my God.

I was crushed. It must have shown, because Dr. Conley started explaining that I shouldn't worry about how I looked, how everyone had something they didn't like about their face. Why, he himself had had terrible acne as a teenager, and that had made him feel awful. Acne, was he serious? How could my problem actually be compared to acne. Any hope I'd allowed myself died right then.

My despair worsened a few days later when I went to

the library with my father. While he stayed downstairs and picked among the fiction, I went upstairs to the nonfiction department and secretly looked up books on plastic surgery. In the middle of giant, outdated tomes, I found photographs of the pedestal procedure. The people in the photographs looked like freaks. With their own skin and muscle sewn to disjointed parts of their anatomy, they looked like illustrations of some brilliant medieval torture device. Worst of all, the final outcome made them look exactly like what they were: people with alien bits of flesh sewn to them. To my eye, many of the people used as examples looked even worse afterward. I was so frightened I could not get my breath, and I had to sit down with my head between my legs until the buzzing was gone from my ears. Was this what my life was going to be? I felt utterly without hope, completely alone and without any chance of ever being loved. Feeling as if I had uncovered some horrible secret, I went downstairs to meet my father.

As we drove home together, he asked me what was wrong, but I couldn't tell him. At home I went to my room, where I wanted desperately to cry, but even the tears were numbed back. I lay frozen on my bed watching a spider walking back and forth on the ceiling until my mother called me for dinner. For the first time I wished I were dead.

Relief came in two unexpected ways. The first occurred some months later, toward the end of eighth grade, when Kelly, a girl I had met at the stable, had to move to another state. Unable to take her horse, an ex-racehorse named

Sure Swinger, she arranged with my parents to give him to me. I'd never understood just how quickly, how splendidly and suddenly, reality could change, how you could look down at the shoes on your own two feet and wonder if they were real.

The second form of comfort came in the person of Dr. Daniel Baker, a younger associate of Dr. Conley's. He and some other doctors were working on a reconstruction technique involving microsurgery, a very new field at the time, to graft vascularized free flaps. This "state of the art" surgery involved taking a large chunk of soft tissue, probably from my groin, and sewing the whole thing, veins and all, onto the jaw area. This not only dispensed with the cumbersome, multistage pedestal procedure, but it also offered a greater chance that the graft would survive, because the new tissue would have its own blood supply. Dr. Baker explained that it would be best to wait another year or so, perhaps until I was sixteen, so that I could grow some more first. I would have to have a major operation followed by lesser ones to shape the graft, but Dr. Baker seemed to think there was a good chance of achieving "a near-normal jaw line."

I can still see my father's reaction as he stood in the corner of Dr. Baker's office, listening to his words and beaming. I had never mentioned my fears concerning my face to my father, and in my solipsism I had never thought that he might share my unhappiness. The halo of joy that surrounded him now was a revelation to me. His joy made me feel better, though it also occurred to me that my face must really be as bad as I feared if he found such relief at the possibility of this surgery.

Maybe life was going to be all right after all. Maybe this wasn't my actual face at all but the face of some interloper, some ugly intruder, and my "real" face, the one I was meant to have all along, was within reach. I began to imagine my "original" face, the one free from all deviation, all error. I believed that if none of this had happened to me, I would have been beautiful. I looked in the mirror closely and imagined the lower half of my face filled out, normal. Reaching my hand up, I covered my chin and jaw, and yes, even I could see that the rest of my face really was beautiful. As soon as I took my hand away, the ugliness of the lower half canceled out the beauty of the upper half, but now this didn't matter so much: it was all going to be "fixed."

What would it be like to walk down the street and be able to trust that no one would say anything nasty to me? My only clues were from Halloween and from the winter, when I could wrap up the lower half of my face in a scarf and talk to people who had no idea that my beauty was a lie, a trick that would be exposed the minute I had to take off the scarf. To feel that confidence without the threat of exposure — how could I possibly want anything more? If they thought I was beautiful, and here I could almost not dare to think such a thing, they might even love me. Me, as an individual, as a person.

I'd rationalized my own desires for so long that I was genuinely perplexed as to whether this sudden and glorious sense of relief at the prospect of having my face fixed was valid. Was the love that I'd guarded against for so long going to be the reward for my suffering? I had put a great deal of effort into accepting that my life would be without love and beauty in order to be comforted by Love and Beauty. Did my eager willingness to grasp the idea of "fixing" my face somehow invalidate all those years of toil? I did not trust the idea that happiness could be an option.

For a few months I settled into a routine of living what felt like three separate lives. Days were filled with school, where I tried to be as fiercely intelligent as I could. My armor would be my academic prowess, from which I was developing a superiority complex as earnestly built as it was defensively acquired. In my second life I still lived in a violent fantasy in which I had no choice but to appreciate the life I led in reality, the one in which my face seemed a frivolous thing compared with a land mine or a pogrom. The third life took place after school, and all day during the summer, when I went to my horse, Swinger, with whom I was conducting nothing less than a romantic relationship.

I knew his whole being. There was not one part of his body I could not touch, not one part of his personality I did not know at least as well as my own. When we went on long rides through the woods, I would tell him everything I knew and then explain why I loved him so much, why he was special, different from other horses, how I would take care of him for the rest of his life, never leave him or let anyone harm him. After the ride I would take him to graze in an empty field. I would lie down on his broad bare back and think I was the luckiest girl alive, his weight shifting beneath me as he moved toward the next bite of grass. Sometimes I took him to the stream and laughed as he pawed at the water, screaming in delight when he tried to lie down in it. Best of all was when I happened to find him lying down in his stall. Carefully, so as not to spook him, I'd creep in and lie down on top of his giant body, his great animal heat and breath rising up to swallow my own smaller heat and less substantial air.

NINE

World of Unknowing

⌒

WHEN SCHOOL STARTED AGAIN, MY NINTH-GRADE
English class began reading poetry. Our first assignment
was Theodore Roethke's "My Papa's Waltz." I read it duti-
fully the night before class and recognized in the image of
the father's dirty hand and the boy's dizzying bewilderment something beautiful and important, something that
vaguely had to do with my own family. And as I recognized myself, I also realized the precision of language; I
knew that the poem could not have been written in any
way except exactly as it had been. The poem's power over
me came from the author's unassailable ability to say what
felt so right and true. I think I already understood that
beauty was somehow related to mystery, but for the first
time I saw that mystery was not just a cause but also a
natural result of beauty. I tried to say all this in class the
next day, but my teacher wanted us to talk about whether
or not the boy loved his father. As we spent the forty
minutes debating along those lines, what I knew about my

love for my own father seemed to grow only more distant and closed off.

Earlier in my childhood, when my father came home late at night, he would shout greetings to everybody as he came through the door, and Sarah and the dogs and I would go running to greet him. But as we got older we were less interested in this ritual, and eventually only the dogs would get up to greet him, while Sarah and I tossed off distracted greetings from our seats in front of the television set. One evening I had a terrible premonition of the time, after Sarah and I had grown up and moved out and the dogs were long dead, when he would come home and there would be only his own voice echoing emptily up the stairs. I felt a strange chill, a hollow and unspeakably sad chill, almost as if I had seen a ghost. From that day on I made a point, even when I didn't particularly feel like it, of greeting him at the top of the stairs. I saw this in terms of my future absence from his life; it never occurred to me that he would ever be absent from mine.

Just seven or eight months after that premonition, I had my first experience of death. Only four months after I received him, Swinger developed an infection in his hoof. I watched carefully as Gene, one of the few regular adult employees of the stable, gave Swinger the prescribed penicillin injection in his neck. Then I went down to the tack room to put something away. After finishing my chore, I turned back to the ring, where Gene was leading Swinger. I was about to crack a joke like, "What do you think you're doing with my horse?" when I realized something was terribly wrong. Swinger was falling down and trying to get back up, only to fall down again. Finally he could not get back up at all.

A crowd had gathered and everyone was yelling and shouting and trying to rouse him, but his legs were sticking almost straight out and trembling and his eyes were rolling into the back of his head. Gene shouted at me to run and get a blanket from the barn. I tore away and fumbled to get the blanket off its rack. With it in hand, I ran back to the ring, but as I got closer I saw that everyone was just standing there, not shouting anymore. Gene reached the gate before me. With one arm, he held it shut and wouldn't let me back in. I looked at him, dropped the blanket, and burst into tears, all the while strangely aware of the melodrama of it all, as if I were remembering this scene from a movie I'd seen. The shot was of Gene's strong and hairy arm barring my way, of everyone standing so silent, of Swinger's huge dark body on the ground. Although I had never liked Gene very much, I allowed him to hold me as I sobbed. I smelled the sweat on his clothes and looked toward Swinger and saw the slow line of urine seeping into the lightly colored dust. I had read that you peed and defecated when you died, and now I knew it was true.

I couldn't bring myself to call my mother to tell her what had happened — I asked someone else to call for me. When she came to pick me up, for some reason I was frightened by the prospect of her reaction: would she be mad? Naturally she was very sympathetic, but I couldn't shake the feeling of shame. When we got home I went wordlessly down to my room and watched television in a stupor of grief. Finally I heard my father come home, shout his usual greeting, and walk up the stairs into the kitchen, which was above my room. I could hear my parents' footsteps above me, and I knew she was telling him. I listened as he walked down the stairs then silently over the thick rug toward my room. I felt the same sense of shame I'd experienced with my mother, not unlike the times he'd visited me in the hospital. He offered his condolences and kissed my ears, which tickled and annoyed me so that I pushed him away, and then left.

My mourning was so untouchable that I had no clue as to what to do with it. Perhaps Swinger had died because I loved him too much: what other reason could there be? Why else would God allow the being I loved more than any other living thing in the world, including myself, to die like that? If this had some kind of meaning, if I was supposed to learn some lesson, I didn't care. Ever since the moment when Gene stopped me at the gate, I had been unable to stop observing everything from an untraceable distance. Even as I felt the worst pain I could ever remember feeling, a sense of the drama of my situation crept in, and there, in front of my private audience, I played my role of the hapless and ill-fated lover once again.

I was stricken over Swinger's death for several months, but time eventually did perform its healing task, and gradually I became excited at the prospect of getting another horse, promised by my parents. I knew that money was still an issue and that this new horse might not materialize straight away, but I knew they would not go back on their word. But sometime after Christmas my mother received a phone call from my dad's boss, explaining that he had gone to the hospital because of stomach pains. My first reaction was that this would put a wrench in my new-horse plans. My mother was certain he was only being a hypochondriac, that it was nothing at all. Maybe it was his ulcer acting up again and he was just overreacting. But he was still in the hospital the next day — they were keeping him for tests — and he was there the day after that and the next day, too. My mother started visiting him every day, yet the rest of us stayed behind, assuming he would be out the very next day.

The weeks turned into months, and each day we received a new report on my father's health. He had pancreatitis: no one would say if he would get better or not. One day toward the end of March, my mother came home and told us they'd put my father on oxygen. Inwardly I shuddered. Everything I knew about hospitals told me that this was a bad thing. My father was going to die, and as bad as this knowledge was, it was made worse by my notion that I was the only one who understood it. My family was not the sort to openly discuss things. Though we all must have been hurting, we did not speak of my father except with a forced optimism.

Just before my father had gone into the hospital, he'd bought an expensive hand-tailored suit, and he'd joined a record club, which began sending recordings of Beethoven's complete works. The fancy suit that he'd been so proud of — the source of a fight between him and my mother because of its price — hung unworn in his closet.

And each week a new selection of records arrived, wrapped in plastic, which we piled unopened next to the phonograph in the living room.

My father's bedroom was a disaster area, filled with stray papers and dirty socks and odd cups and occasional forks. I went in and surveyed it all just as I'd done when I was younger and he was away at work, but now I was looking for something else. I had no idea what. Before, I'd wanted some kind of clue as to what it was to be my father, what it was to be a man, to be an adult. Now I was looking for something that would explain my father's life to me. I couldn't find it.

Back in the living room, I could no longer bear the sight of the unopened records. Ripping the plastic off, I put on one after another of the records and listened for five or six hours. I wanted to see why my father loved Beethoven so much. Finally I fell asleep lying there on the carpet; I was awakened by the dogs barking at my mother's return. Hurriedly, I put the records away. I'm not sure why, but I didn't want anyone to know I'd listened to them.

The whole time he was in the hospital, I went to visit my father only once. Even after all these years, I don't understand why we stayed away. Were we so adrift in our own sea of grief that we were able to convince ourselves that it was better this way? He grew more and more disoriented. My mother reported that he kept pointing to a pin she wore, a pin he'd bought for her before they were married, pointing to it as if he were picking it out again for the first time. He became paranoid, talking about Germans and the dogs the Germans had set on him when he was a prisoner of war during the Second World War. He'd been a pilot in the RAF, and we had a dashing, fuzzy photo of him in his flak suit, smiling at an unseen person casting a shadow near his feet. It was easy to forget about that part of my father's life because he never spoke of it. I remember once watching *Hogan's Heroes* while he was in the room. He was appalled that a television comedy would be set in a German POW camp. Knowing nothing of his war experience at the time, I told him I thought he was overreacting. It pained me to think that now, near the end of his life, he was reliving this nightmare, as alone as he had been the first time. We spent the next couple of weeks waiting. Every time the phone rang, the whole house went silent.

I was dreading the inevitable phone call, mostly because I did not want to see the rest of my family's reactions to it. I knew that Sarah would break down and cry, but I didn't know what everyone else would do. I wanted my father to die and for there to be no fuss, no outbreaks, no displays. I was terrified.

When the call did come at last, one afternoon some six weeks before my sixteenth birthday, my mother was on the phone at the far end of the kitchen, my brother Nicholas was sitting at one end of the table, Sarah was sitting at the other end, and I was standing in the doorway. Susie was away at college and Sean was living in California. Sarah, Nicholas, and I remained motionless as we listened to my mother speak, thanking the doctor for all he had done, and when she got off she told us matter-of-factly and very sadly what we already knew. To my great surprise, it wasn't Sarah who cried but Nicholas. He put his head down on the table and wept, and all I could think of was that I didn't expect this, just as I didn't expect Sarah to sit there so calmly. I turned my head and looked at the painting on the wall next to me. It was a head of Christ painted by Sean, one I'd passed several thousand times, yet I felt I was seeing it for the first time. I'd never noticed how much brown he'd used in the thorns, how much gold for the skin. It all seemed so very odd, so very distant, and I was reminded how I'd seen the ceiling in Dr. Woolf's office so clearly that last day there. Was this feeling that everything was happening for the first time real, did grief heighten vision, or was it only an illusion, a way to distance myself from what was happening?

Along with sadness, a sense of relief followed my father's death. At least we weren't waiting anymore. Also we were going to receive some money from the insurance company, and the prospect of paying off some bills and finally getting ahead offered a guilty sense of pleasure. I was sitting in the kitchen a couple of days after my dad's funeral. Perhaps we were still in shock, but Sarah and I were laughing hysterically over a new joke we'd heard, and just as we were in the thick of it, the phone rang. It was my surgeon, Dr. Baker. I was shocked to hear his voice, for he was nothing less than a monumental figure in my life, but when he offered his condolences, all I could do was jauntily reply, as if he'd just apologized for stepping on my shoe, "Oh, that's all right, it doesn't matter." As soon as I hung up the phone I realized what I'd done. But as I told Sarah about the call, the two of us burst out again in uncontrollable laughter.

*   *   *

That June, a few weeks after my sixteenth birthday, I went into New York University Medical Center for my first reconstructive operation, my first microvascularized free flap. I liked this hospital: it was newer and better staffed than Columbia Presbyterian, and I was no longer relegated to the children's ward. My ward was devoted solely to plastic surgery, and I was shocked to see how many people were having their noses done, their faces lifted.

The woman in the bed next to me was having her breast reconstructed after a mastectomy, and she insisted on telling me all about her scars and her feelings of ugliness. I had no patience with her lament: her face was beautiful, and she had a husband who brought her a dozen red roses. It was true she was missing a breast, but I didn't see how that mattered as long as she had these other things. No one could see her missing breast when she walked down the street, no one would make fun of her or think she was ugly, and someone loved her. I listened to her and realized that she was genuinely suffering, that her feelings of ugliness consumed her as much as mine consumed me, but she was mistaken, I thought, for there was no doubt she was beautiful. Her problems lay in her perception. Talking with her only strengthened my conviction of the importance in this world of having a beautiful face. Still, I liked her, and I liked being treated as an adult by another adult. We ordered out for Chinese food for what I kept calling "my last meal." "No, no, don't say that," she tried to reassure me. I just couldn't get her to see that I was joking; I could tell she was new at this hospital stuff.

The anesthetist came to see me that night and decided

that it might be hard to intubate me — insert a breathing tube into my windpipe — so he would do it while I was awake. It didn't sound like a big deal, and I didn't think twice about it.

The next morning, however, as I lay dazed on the stretcher, I heard them talking about nasal intubation. Immediately I started worrying, and for good reason. First they tried passing a tube up one nostril. It didn't hurt, but when it reached the back of my throat I gagged. Worse, they kept prying my mouth open to see where it was going. They couldn't reach it, so they pulled it out and tried the other nostril. By now I was upset, but I lay as still as I could. That nostril didn't work either, so they decided to go straight through my mouth. This required prying my mouth open and keeping it open, which hurt like hell, but worse was that at each attempt to pass the tube, my airway was temporarily blocked and I couldn't breathe, which put me into a panic. The pre-op medications were slowing my reactions and making it hard for me to understand what was going on.

I instinctively started to struggle, reaching up and trying to push their strangling hands away from me. When two nurses came and held me down, I started to cry and struggle even more, but they only held me tighter and kept pushing the tube down my throat. They must have sedated me even further, because my reactions grew more sluggish and all reality ceased to exist outside of the confines of my stretcher. I begged them to stop, but no one responded. This upset me most of all. No one cared, or seemed to, and I wailed even louder.

Suddenly everyone seemed to disappear and I was left

in peace, floating, but still crying hard. I looked up and there was Dr. Baker, looking down at me. He reached out his hand and placed it on my forehead, replicating the gesture I'd received during my very first operation. I was calmed instantly, as if all my sorrows existed within that one single point on my forehead. I remember having a surreal vision of myself as if I were a bystander in the room, looking at the clownish cap they'd made me wear to hold back my hair, the clear, greenish tube arching awkwardly out of my mouth, and then I was asleep.

When I awoke I was in a lot of pain, but the pain was in my hip, where the graft came from, far away from my face, my "self," so it was easier to deal with. As soon as I remembered why I'd had an operation, I reached up to touch my face. I felt a large, warm, very soft mass where there used to be an indent. I felt a complicated trail of stitches, and near my ear was a drain. Turning my head, I tried to see my reflection in the metal bed rails, but I could only glimpse a distorted image of something I didn't recognize as my own face. When my mother came to visit, she asked how I felt and I responded with a question.

"What does it look like?"

"Well, dear, it's a bit hard to tell. It's very swollen."

"But do you think it will be all right?"

"Well, he's definitely filled it out. But it's so swollen now, you have to wait and see."

I didn't want to wait. After she had gone I asked a nurse to describe it to me. "You have to understand that it's very swollen and bruised. It will change." I asked for a mirror.

Sitting up was too painful, so I lay there and held the mirror above me, staring up at an image I only vaguely recognized. "Swollen" was an understatement. This new thing on my face was huge, almost touching my collarbone. What repulsed me most was a large strip of foreign skin, much paler than my facial skin, running along the lower half of my new jaw line. Surrounded by dozens of minute stitches, it looked just like what it was, a patch. The rest of my face looked horrible as well, all pale and puffy, and my hair was full of dried blood. I handed the mirror back to the nurse, thanked her, and went back to sleep.

When I woke up again I tried not to think about my face. I tried to remind myself that it had been only a few hours since the surgery was finished, and I couldn't judge the end result by what I had seen in the mirror. There would be more operations to revise the graft, to remove the extra skin, which had been purposely placed there to allow space for all the swelling, and to allow the graft to be monitored.

The next few hours were crucial, and it was important that the graft keep its blood supply. Every hour a nurse walked in and touched me there to feel its warmth, then poked me to test capillary reaction. I saw the hand coming near my face, but I couldn't feel a thing. I wasn't the least bit concerned with whether the graft would survive; I assumed it would. Far more important to me was whether or not the operation had been a horrible mistake in the first place. I knew better than to expect perfection, yet I had not anticipated how *foreign* it would look. I shut down, tried not to think about it. When I did think about it, I projected my thinking forward to the next operation, the one that would fix this one.

I turned my attention to the process of healing. At first lying still had been no problem, but now I was getting cramps in my legs. To relieve the cramps I had to move my legs, and that sent shooting pains through the muscles in my torso. I felt as if I were in some kind of science fiction movie in which people are kept prisoner within bizarre, invisible force fields. At the same time, I didn't really mind the pain. Pain, if nothing else, was honest and open — you knew exactly what you were dealing with.

After the first few hours I was taken out of Intensive Care and sent to Special Care, which was one rung lower on the attention scale. There were three other beds. The one directly across from me was empty. In the one next to that, kitty-corner from my bed, was a girl who, I found out from eavesdropping, was dying from a brain tumor. Relatives came and gave her presents, which she opened with a blank, unknowing face. When she spoke, her words were unintelligible. She would grow frustrated when no one understood her and would throw a tantrum, sending objects flying across the room and toward the bed next to mine, where a teenage boy named Michael was recovering.

Michael's first comment to me was about my stuffed kangaroo, which my mother had bought for me and which all the nurses commented on. He said, dryly, that my kangaroo had usurped his monkey as the cutest toy on the ward. His monkey hung from a bar at arm's length above his bed. I didn't know what *usurped* meant, and when I asked him he laughed. He was only a year older than me, but he seemed to have lived a whole life already.

Michael would reach up to the bar hanging over his bed and use his arms to hoist himself up. He didn't wear a pajama top, so when his back was momentarily off the bed, I could see his muscles flex and the red lines indented into the pale skin of his back from lying on the sheets too long. He told me he'd dived off the top of a two-story building into a pool and had hurt his back.

"Why'd you do that?"

"I don't know," he answered, looking up at the ceiling. "It was a friend's pool," he said after a moment, as if that should somehow clarify the situation.

Whenever he spoke, he sounded slightly bored, slightly distant. But he talked with me quite a bit over the next couple of days, and I always felt privileged that he was speaking to me at all. If he were at school, would he be one of the boys who made fun of me? I stole sideways glances at him, his long wavy hair, the stubble on his chin and upper lip, and thought that, probably, yes, he would be. Yet here we were lying next to each other, both of us in a lot of pain, and I knew that here he would never dream of saying anything mean to me. I felt faintly triumphant. Someone from that "other world" had come over to mine.

One night Michael refused to take a particular pill, and the doctor came to argue with him about it. Michael fought with the doctors all the time, always questioning them and refusing to do things he didn't want to do; he was my complete opposite, for I still looked for praise as a "model patient." It was the middle of the night and the main overhead lights were off. His curtain was drawn, and I saw Michael's and the doctor's shadows thrown against the yellow curtain. The pill Michael was refusing to take was something he needed for his stomach. The doctor was explaining that when you spent so much time lying down, your digestive juices didn't work well, and this pill would counteract that. Michael kept refusing, his voice rising in protest, which I didn't understand at all. Why didn't he just take it? Then, inexplicably, he started crying and screamed at the doctor to leave. As the doctor left, I lay there looking at Michael's shadow, wondering if I should say something.

A few minutes later a nurse came to empty his urine catheter bag. I knew he had one — I had one too — but I'd never thought about how it might work with a man. The nurse didn't close the curtain properly, and when I looked over I saw for the first time an adult male's penis, this one being pushed up and held falsely erect by the tube inserted into it. It came as a shock because it was the first time I acknowledged that Michael, at the age of seventeen, was permanently paralyzed, all because of a stupid trick that took him ten seconds to perform.

I couldn't help but compare his situation to my own. My life was "different" from most people's, but it was essentially my own. I hated the face I remembered having a few days ago, and I knew nothing of the face I had now except that I feared it. But it existed, and I had only to look at it to know what it was. Michael had lost something he was never going to get back; my face had only changed into the next shape it was meant to have. I could not dare to think I might actually want or like that shape, but I had a sudden realization that to have it at all meant something.

Two days later I was transferred to a regular ward. As I was wheeled away I promised Michael I would come visit him, but I never did. As soon as I was back on the ward filled with nose jobs and jowl tucks, I grew fearful of my distorted face again and put Michael and his predicament out of my mind. I was walking to the bathroom by myself now, and each time I opened the door I saw my own face reflected back at me. Was that really me? I knew it had to be, but how could it possibly relate to the person I thought I was, or wanted to be? I considered the whole operation a failure, and when the doctors came around and told me how well it was healing, how good it looked, my heart sank. We were speaking two different languages; if this looked good, then what I thought would look good must be an impossible dream. I felt stupid for having had any expectations or hopes at all.

When I got home, I thought of Michael again and again. Did he ever reimagine himself standing on that roof or try to remember what it was like to not know his fate for just one split second longer? If he didn't, I did it for him. I'd close my eyes to feel the height, see the bright blue of the pool winking below me, bend my legs, and feel the pull in my calves as I jumped up and then down, falling from one world of unknowing into the next one of perpetual regret.

TEN

The Habits of Self-Consciousness

~

IT WAS ONLY WHEN I GOT HOME FROM THE HOSPI-
tal that I permitted myself to look more closely at my new
face. It was still extremely swollen (it would be months
before it went down), and a long thin scar ran the length of
it. In the middle of the scar was the island of pale skin from
my hip. Placing my hand over the swollen and discolored
parts, I tried to imagine how my face might look once it
was "better." If I positioned the angle of my face, the angle
of my hand, and the angle of the mirror all just right, it
looked okay.

Actually, in my mind, my face looked even better than
okay, it looked beautiful. But it was a beauty that existed in
the future, a possible future. As it was, I hated my face. I
turned my thoughts inward again, and this strange fantasy
of beauty became something very private, a wish I would
have been ashamed to let anyone in on. Primarily it was a

fantasy of relief. When I tried to imagine being beautiful, I could only imagine living without the perpetual fear of being alone, without the great burden of isolation, which is what feeling ugly felt like.

The beginning of high school was a couple of months away. Each day I checked my face in private, wondering what I would look like by my first day at a new school. I expected to have a second "revising" operation before school started, but as it turned out I would have to wait at least another three months, a span of time that seemed useless and insurmountable. What was the point, if I still had to walk into school that first day looking like this?

There was only one solution, and that was to stop caring. I became pretentious. I picked out thick books by Russian authors and carted them around with me. Sometimes I even read them. *Anna Karenina, The Brothers Karamazov, Dead Souls.* I read *Jude the Obscure* simply because I liked the title, and anything else that sounded difficult and deep. Often I missed the subtle nuances of these books, but they presented a version of the world in which honor and virtue and dedication to the truth counted. The stories comforted me, though it didn't escape my attention that these qualities were ascribed primarily to men. The women might be virtuous as well, but their physical beauty was crucial to the story.

On the first day of school I rode the bus, entered my strange homeroom, and went through my day of classes as invisibly as possible. By now my hair was long, past my shoulders, and I walked around with my head bent, my dark blond hair covering half my face. Having decided against seeking anything as inconsequential as social status, I spent the days observing my peers with a perfectly calibrated air of disinterest. I remained the outsider, like so many of the characters I had read about, and in this role I found great comfort. Doubtless I was more keenly aware of the subtleties of the various dramas and social dances of my classmates than they were themselves.

For the most part I was left alone. People were a bit more mature, and it was rare that anyone openly made fun of me. But I was still braced for the teasing. Every time I saw someone looking at me, I expected the worst. Usually they just looked the other way and didn't register much interest one way or the other. Then, just as I would start to relax, to let my guard down, some loudmouthed boy would feel a need to point out to his friends how ugly I was.

One day when I went to my English class, I found a copy of Hesse's *Siddhartha,* his version of the story of the Buddha, lying on my chair. My notions of Buddhism were sketchy at best, but the opening pages immediately reminded me of the messages of grace, dignity, and light that I'd first encountered in those Christian publications, which had long since ceased arriving in the mail. I'd almost forgotten about my quest for enlightenment, imagining my momentous meeting with the great guru. Now, after so much time and so much loss, I took it as a sign that someone had left this book on my chair. Desire and all its painful complications, I decided, was something I should and would be free of.

*   *   *

Two months after school started, the long-awaited revision operation was scheduled. I started focusing on the upcoming date, believing that my life would finally get started once I had the face I was "supposed" to have. Logically I knew that this was only one of many operations, but surely it would show promise, offer a hint of how it was all going to turn out.

When I woke up in recovery the day after the operation, I looked up to see a nurse wearing glasses leaning over me. Cautiously I looked for my reflection in her glasses. There I was, my hair messed and my face pale and, as far as I could tell, looking exactly the same as before. I reached up and felt the suture line. A few hours later, when I was recovered enough to walk unaided to the bathroom, I took each careful step toward the door and geared myself up to look in the mirror. Apart from looking like I'd just gotten over a bad case of flu, I looked just the same. The patch of paler skin was gone, but the overall appearance of my face was no different from before.

I blamed myself for the despair I felt creeping in; again it was a result of having expectations. I must guard against having any more. After all, I still had it pretty good by global standards. "I have food," I told myself. "I have a place to sleep." So what if my face was ugly, so what if other people judged me for this. That was their problem, not mine. This line of reasoning offered less consolation than it had in the past, but it distanced me from what was hurting most, and I took this as a sign that I was getting better at detaching myself from my desires.

When I returned to school I had resolved that my face

was actually an asset. It was true I hated it and saw it as the cause of my isolation, but I interpreted it as some kind of lesson. I had taught myself about reincarnation, how the soul picks its various lives with the intent of learning more and more about itself so that it may eventually break free of the cycle of karma. Why had my soul chosen this particular life, I asked myself; what was there to learn from a face as ugly as mine? At the age of sixteen I decided it was all about desire and love.

Over the years my perspective on "what it was all about" has shifted, but the most important point then was that there *was* a reason for this happening to me. No longer feeling that I was being punished, as I had during the chemo, I undertook to see my face as an opportunity to find something that had not yet been revealed. Perhaps my face was a gift to be used toward understanding and enlightenment. This was all noble enough, but by equating my face with ugliness, in believing that without it I would never experience the deep, bottomless grief I called ugliness, I separated myself even further from other people, who I thought never experienced grief of this depth. Not that I did not allow others their own suffering. I tried my best to be empathic because I believed it was a "good" emotion. But in actuality I was judge and hangman, disgusted by peers who avoided their fears by putting their energy into things as insubstantial as fashion and boyfriends and gossip.

I tried my best, but for the most part I was as abysmal at seeking enlightenment as I had once been at playing dodge ball. No matter how desperately I wanted to catch that ball, I dropped it anyway. And as much as I wanted to love everybody in school and to waft esoterically into the ether when someone called me ugly, I was plagued with petty desires and secret, evil hates.

I hated Danny in my orchestra class because I had a crush on him and knew that he would never have a crush on me. Anger scared me most of all, and I repressed every stirring. Every time I felt hatred, or any other "bad" thought, I shooed it away with a broom of spiritual truisms. But the more I tried to negate my feelings, the more they crowded in. I not only harbored hatred for Danny even while I had a crush on him, I also hated Katherine, the girl in orchestra *he* had a crush on. Trying to repress that feeling, I found myself hating Katherine's cello, of all things, which she played exquisitely well. The cycle eventually ended with me: I hated myself for having even entertained the absurd notion that someone like Danny could like me.

I didn't begrudge Danny his crush on Katherine. She was pretty and talented, so why shouldn't he want her? I was never going to have anyone want me in that way, so I mustn't desire such a thing; in this way I could be grateful to my face for "helping" me to see the error of earthly desire. This complicated gratitude usually lasted for about five minutes before giving way to depression, plain and simple.

When my father's insurance money came, and before we learned of the accumulated tax debt we owed, my mother generously kept her promise and bought me another horse. Her registered name was even more silly than Sure Swinger, so I simply called her Mare. I kept her at Snowcap, a more professional and better-kept stable than Diamond D. There I undertook learning to ride seriously. I fell in love with Mare just as I had with Swinger, and again I had bad luck. Not long after I got her, she broke her leg while turned out in a field. As she limped pathetically onto the trailor to be taken away, they told me they could sell her as a brood mare, but I knew she was too old for this and would be put down shortly. Again my heart was broken, but this time I saw it in much more self-pitying terms. I told myself that anything I loved was doomed, and even as I was aware of my own overblown melodrama, just as I had been that night I nearly collapsed on the hospital floor, I took a strange comfort in this romantic, tragic role.

Luckily, the owners of Snowcap permitted me to continue on at the barn as their exercise rider. This was ideal. Not only did I get to ride horses for free, sometimes as many as six a day, and gain a great deal of experience in the process, but it also gave my life a center. I withstood school all day, knowing I would go straight to the barn afterward and stay there until eight or nine o'clock at night. The barn became the one place where I felt like myself, and I relished the physicality of riding, performing acts I was good at, feeling a sense of accomplishment. I spent as little time at home as possible.

During tenth grade I had one more operation to work on shaping the free flap, and the results seemed as trivial and ineffectual to me as the last time. The following summer I spent every day with the horses. One day when it was too hot to get very much accomplished, I went along for the ride on an errand with some people from the stable. We got caught in traffic on the main road, and as we crept along at a snail's pace, I looked out the window and got lost in my own world. A bakery storefront, its door set at a very odd angle, caught my attention, reminding me of something I couldn't quite put my finger on. Then I remembered that I had been to this town some ten or twelve years earlier with my father. He loved to go out for a drive on a Sunday and explore the area, and Sarah and I loved to accompany him. We'd stand up in the back seat and sing songs with him, songs from his own distant childhood, so familiar and lovely to him that we could both hear that strange, sad love in his voice as he sang. Unexpectedly, and consciously for the first time since his death, I missed my father.

The one time I had visited him in the hospital, I had had to wait outside in the hallway briefly. The smells and sounds were so familiar — the sweet disinfectant and wax, always an aroma of overcooked food in the background, the metallic clinks of IV poles as they were pushed along the floor on their stands. Yet I was only visiting, passing through. I had felt alone and without purpose, unidentified, not sure how to act. Now, more than a year after his death, I again didn't know how to act. I didn't want to ignore the grief or even get over it, because that would mean I hadn't loved my father. When my horse died, I had cried almost continuously for days. The loss was pure and uncomplicated. Loving my father had been a different matter. I finally and suddenly found myself consumed with a longing for his presence.

I started imagining my father standing next to me in the hospital, visiting me. With all my might I strained to hear the background noises of the hospital, feel the starch of the sheets, and hear my father's footsteps approaching, hear the rustle of his clothes as he stood near me, his cough to see if I was awake. I'd imagine opening my eyes very slowly, very carefully, and try to see him, standing beside my hospital bed. All I could conjure was the vaguest of outlines, a passing detail that only seemed to obscure the rest of him: how his watch fitted on his wrist, how he would trace the edge of his ear with one finger.

Spending as much time as I did looking in the mirror, I thought I knew what I looked like. So it came as a shock one afternoon toward the end of that summer when I went shopping with my mother for a new shirt and saw my face in the harsh fluorescent light of the fitting room. Pulling the new shirt on over my head, I caught a glimpse of my reflection in a mirror that was itself being reflected in a mirror opposite, reversing my face as I usually saw it. I stood there motionless, the shirt only halfway on, my skin extra pale from the lighting, and saw how asymmetrical my face was. How had that happened? Walking up to the mirror, reaching up to touch the right side, where the graft had been put in only a year before, I saw clearly that most of it had disappeared, melted away into nothing. I felt distraught at the sight and even more distraught that it had taken so long to notice. My eyes had been secretly working against me, making up for the asymmetry as it gradually reappeared. This reversed image of myself was the true image, the way other people saw me.

I felt like such a fool. I'd been walking around with a secret notion of promised beauty, and here was the reality. When I saw Dr. Baker a few weeks later, I wanted desperately to ask him what had gone wrong, but I found myself speechless. Besides, I knew that the graft had been reabsorbed by my body — the doctor had warned me it might happen. He spoke of waiting a few years before trying any more big operations, of letting me grow some more. We spoke about a series of minor operations that would make readjustments to what was already there, but there was only vague talk of any new grafts, of putting more soft tissue or bone in place. Sitting in his expensively decorated office, I felt utterly powerless. Realizing I was going to have to change my ideals and expectations was one thing, but knowing what to replace them with was another.

That unexpected revelation in the store's fitting room mirror marked a turning point in my life. I began having overwhelming attacks of shame at unpredictable intervals. The first one came as I was speaking to Hans, my boss at the stable. He was describing how he wanted me to ride a certain horse. I was looking him in the eye as he spoke, and he was looking me in the eye. Out of nowhere came an intense feeling that he shouldn't be looking at me, that I was too horrible to look at, that I wasn't worthy of being looked at, that my ugliness was equal to a great personal failure. Inside I was churning and shrinking, desperate for a way to get out of this. I took the only course of action I knew I was any good at: I acted as if nothing were wrong. Steadying myself, breathing deeply, I kept looking him in the eye, determined that he should know nothing of what I was thinking.

That summer I started riding horses for Hans in local schooling shows. In practices I always wore a helmet with my hair hanging loose beneath it, but etiquette required that during shows my hair be tucked neatly up beneath the helmet, out of sight. I put this off until the very last minute, trying to act casual as I reached for the rubber band and hair net. This simple act of lifting my hair and exposing my face was among the hardest things I ever had to do, as hard as facing Dr. Woolf, harder than facing operations. I gladly would have undergone any amount of physical pain to keep my hair down. No one at the show grounds ever commented to me about it, and certainly no one there was going to make fun of me, but I was beyond that point. By then I was perfectly capable of doing it all to myself.

The habits of self-consciousness, of always looking down and hiding my face behind my hair or my hand, were so automatic by now that I was blind to them. When my mother pointed out these habits to me in the hope of making me stop, telling me they directed even more attention to my face, she might as well have been telling me to change the color of my eyes.

I fantasized about breakthroughs in reconstructive surgery, about winning the lottery and buying my own private island, about being abducted by space aliens who'd fix me up and plop me back down in the midst of a surprised public. And there were still acts of heroism waiting to be thrust upon me, whole busloads of babies to be saved and at least one, there had to be at least one out there, wise older man who would read about my heroism in the papers, fall in love with my inner beauty, and whisk me away from the annoyance of existence as defined by Spring Valley High School.

During the eleventh and twelfth grades I had several small operations. The hospital was the only place on earth where I didn't feel self-conscious. My face was my battle scar, my badge of honor. The people in the plastic surgery ward hated their gorgeously hooked noses, their wise lines, their exquisitely thin lips. Beauty, as defined by society at large, seemed to be only about who was best at looking like everyone else. If *I* had my original face, an undamaged face, *I* would know how to appreciate it, know how to see the beauty of it. Yet each time I was wheeled down to the surgical wing, high on the drugs, I'd think to myself, *Now, now I can start my life, just as soon as I wake up from this operation.* And no matter how disappointed I felt when I woke up and looked in the mirror, I'd simply postpone happiness until the next operation. I knew there would always be another operation, another chance for my life to finally begin.

In the wake of my recurring disappointment I'd often chide myself for thinking I'd ever be beautiful enough, good enough, or worthy enough of someone else's love, let alone my own. Who cared if I loved my own face if no one else was going to? What was beauty for, after all, if not to attract the attention of men, of lovers? When I walked down a street or hallway, sometimes men would whistle at me from a distance, call me *Baby,* yell out and ask me my name. I was thin, I had a good figure, and my long blond hair, when I bothered to brush it, was pretty. I would walk as fast as possible, my head bent down, but sometimes they'd catch up with me, or I'd be forced to pass by them. Their comments would stop instantly when they saw my face, their sudden silence potent and damning.

Life in general was cruel and offered only different types of voids and chaos. The only way to tolerate it, to have any hope of escaping it, I reasoned, was to know my own strength, to defy life by surviving it. Sitting in math class, I'd look around and try to gauge who among my classmates could have lived through this trauma, certain that none of them could. I had already read a great deal about the Holocaust, but now we were reading first-person accounts by Elie Wiesel and Primo Levi in social studies. I was completely transported by their work, and the more I absorbed of their message, the more my everyday life took on a surreal quality. Now everything, *everything,* seemed important. The taste of salt and peanut butter and tomatoes, the smell of car fumes, the small ridge of snow on the inside sill of a barely open window. I thought that this was how to live in the present moment, to resee the world: continuously imagine a far worse reality. At these moments, the life I was leading seemed unimportant, uncomplicated. Sometimes I could truly find refuge in the world of my private senses, but just as often I disingenuously affected a posture of repose, using it as a weapon against people I envied and feared, as a way of feeling superior to and thus safe from them.

After the section on the Holocaust, my social studies class moved on to art history. One day I walked into class late and found the lights off. My teacher was just about to show slides. Giacometti's sculptures flashed on the wall, their elongated arms simultaneously pointing toward and away from the world, while their long legs held them tall and gracefully but tenuously. Next were de Chirico's paintings, with the shadows from unseen others falling directly across the paths of the visible. I had seen Munch's "The Scream" and had identified it with my own occasional desire to let out a howl, but it was only at that moment, sitting in that darkened classroom, that I understood the figure might not be screaming himself but shielding his ears from and dropping his mouth open in shock at the sound of someone, or something, else's loud, loud lament. Matisse's paintings seemed to be about how simple it was to see the world in a beautiful way. Picasso's were about how complex, how difficult, beauty was.

The poems we read in English class had similar effects on me. My taste was not always sophisticated, but I did read poetry by Keats, Emily Dickinson, and Wallace Stevens, which moved me in ways I couldn't understand. It was, in part, the very lack of understanding that was so moving. I would read Keats's "Ode to a Nightingale" and feel that something important and necessary was being said here, but the moment I tried to examine the words, dissect the sentences, the meaning receded.

Senior year I applied to and was accepted at Sarah

Lawrence College with a generous scholarship. Not sure what to do with my life, I decided to work toward medical school. The day senior class yearbook photos were taken, I purposefully cut school, and I threw away all the subsequent notices warning that unless I attended the makeup shoot, my photo would not appear in the yearbook.

ELEVEN

Cool

〜

CERTAIN PEOPLE GO THROUGH RADICAL OUTWARD changes their freshman year of college. This is especially true at Sarah Lawrence, with an enrollment of only eight hundred and a program decidedly focused on liberal arts. The college is only an hour from Spring Valley, so my mother drove me there. She helped me carry boxes up to my dorm room, said good-bye, and drove away. From across the parking lot outside my window I could hear a Herman's Hermits song blaring out, "Something tells me I'm into something good." I took it as an omen. For days beforehand I'd been a nervous wreck, but suddenly I felt I belonged. It was an unusual, curious feeling.

Sarah Lawrence is something of a satellite of New York City's Lower East Side. Some students dressed entirely in black or sported bizarre haircuts indicating the overzealous use of a razor blade, while others wore, with enviable grace and style, exotic, ruined clothes that looked as if they'd washed up on shore after the *Titanic*'s New Year's

Eve party. Everyone cultivated an air of being an outsider, beyond it all, utterly cool. Rather naively, I fell for these appearances instantly, was completely seduced by them. I was shocked to discover that rather than snubbing me, everyone was extraordinarily nice and even interested in me. I was amazed to observe myself so at ease, ready and able to make contact with people. I'd had some friends before college, but they were people I spent time with more than true friends. I would never have considered showing my private self to them. Here, within hours I was having intense discussions about life, art, all the topics I'd been craving for so long.

Yet for all the deep conversations, one's looks still were of paramount importance. Only the aesthetic had changed. In many ways the fashion of cool was every bit as rigorous and unforgiving as the fashion of fitting in had been in high school, only here the rigor depended upon a higher degree of individuality. With amazing predictability — predictability that we the inductees of cool would have scorned had anyone tried to point it out — the freshman class went through its first-semester transformations. I was no exception.

Some of us, after Thanksgiving break, left our embarrassing old chinos and Docksiders at home, and arrived back on campus completely vamped out in retro-punk: dyed magenta hair and green fingernails and long black skirts. Others went for oversized dresses from their grandmother's closets, strange little hats with feathers, pearl necklaces that hung to their navels. Still others went for the sex-toy look: ripped jeans over lace stockings and T-shirts with collars and sleeves tantalizingly torn off. I went with the I-don't-care-I'm-an-artist look, which required that everything I wore come from the Bargain Box, the local thrift store, and cost no more than a dollar-fifty. Extra points went to anything I found lying on the street.

At the heart of this antifashion statement was poetry. Still set on going to medical school, I had signed up for the required science courses, but I had to fill out my schedule with something in the humanities. My mother urged me to take one of the writing workshops the school is well known for, and, deciding that fiction would be too much work, I chose a poetry course. My instructor was a man named John Skoyles, and by the end of the first semester I was hooked.

Reading and writing poetry brought together everything that had ever been important to me. I could still dwell in the realm of the senses, but now I had a discipline, a form for them. Rather than a way to create my own private life and shun the world, the ability to perceive was now a way to enter the world. Language itself, words and images, could be wrought and shaped into vessels for the truth and beauty I had so long hungered for. Most amazing, one could fail, one could make mistake after mistake and learn from each one.

Poetry became a religion for me. I was a fanatic. I'd pull people into a corner and say, without any sense of irony, "You have to hear this, it will change your life." I'd recite anything from Rilke to Ashbery, certain that the deep wonder and awe I felt from these poems would be immediately apparent. I recognized this wonder and awe as intimately connected to the feelings I'd discovered while recovering from chemotherapy sessions, when to simply "be" was reason enough for joy. Now I knew that joy was a kind of fearlessness, a letting go of expectations that the world should be anything other than what it was. And I felt I'd at last discovered the means with which to actively seek out this kind of being, this kind of beauty.

By the end of my freshman year I'd gained a reputation as one of the better poets on campus, which aided the development of my artistic persona. How trivial to actually *think* about one's appearance. The attire of my fellow scruffy artists told the world to recognize them as geniuses too preoccupied to care about anything as mundane as clothes. But for me, dressing as if I didn't care was an attempt not to care, to show the world I wasn't concerned with what it thought of my face. In my carefully orchestrated shabbiness, I was hoping to beat the world to the finish line by showing that I already knew I was ugly. Still, all the while, I was secretly hoping that in the process some potential lover might accidentally notice I was wearing my private but beautiful heart on my stained and fraying sleeve.

In truth there was little danger of meeting someone who might actually desire me, and not just because of my looks. The female-to-male ratio at school was three to one, and much of the male third of the population was, for varying reasons, unavailable. I was free to develop my eccentric ways and thoughts without any threat to my most basic assumptions about myself, my most intimate definitions of what constituted my personality, however painful those definitions may otherwise have been.

The next summer I was looking forward to a second free-flap operation, but it wasn't to be. My mother had to leave her job at the nursing home, which meant I no longer had medical insurance. And to ease her financial burden, she had decided to sell the house, which required a great deal of repairs and general sorting out. After weeks of filling out forms and spending hours on the telephone on hold, I eventually received Medicaid. I went to see Dr. Baker, and together we decided to postpone surgery until the following summer.

The house was sold early in the fall of my sophomore year. For years our poor old dilapidated house had been nothing but an embarrassment, and I'd underestimated its value as a reliable source of comfort, as a place I could always go. Now, to my surprise, I missed it. I experienced a strange kind of orphanhood, a displacement that worked its way into my writing. The word *home* kept cropping up in my poems. When school vacations came around, I'd often spend them as the guest of friends instead of at my mother's new, smaller apartment.

In sharp contrast to high school, I now possessed a large number of varied and decidedly wonderful friends, whom I valued immeasurably. Through them I discovered what it was to love people. There was an art to it, I discovered, which was not really all that different from the love that is necessary in the making of art. It required the effort of always seeing them for themselves and not as I wished them to be, of always striving to see the truth of them.

My vanity allowed me to be proud of my many different types of friends. I was on equally good terms with politically radical and openly hedonistic people, friends who were concerned deeply with the spiritual and those who could not care less about it. Generally, they didn't mix with each other, and often one would be sincerely surprised to discover that I spent time outside of his or her particular group, though most shared the quality of being on the fringe. To be on the fringe at a school as fringy as Sarah Lawrence was itself an accomplishment, but it was this very quality that I loved most about my friends. They wore their mantles as "outsiders" with pride, whether because of their politics, their sexuality, or anything else that makes a person feel outside of the norm. Their self-definition was the very thing that put me at ease with them. I didn't feel judged. I felt acceptance I had never experienced before and was able to genuinely open myself to the love they offered.

As sophomore year drew to a close, I went to see Dr. Baker about setting up the next operation. I was full of hope, but as it turned out, Dr. Baker had far too much work right then to do the operation himself. He was handing me over to a team of two surgeons at St. Vincent's Hospital, down in Greenwich Village. As I waited in Dr. Baker's office, these two new doctors walked in, examined me, and left. Dr. Baker assured me that they were very capable.

Free-flap operations are six to eight hours long, and I felt that I *should* be understanding of how much of Dr. Baker's time it would take, that I should just go along and let these strange doctors take over. "I'm still your doctor," he assured me, but I felt completely cowed, as if I didn't have the right to speak up and voice my fears. I wanted to know if this change had anything to do with my being on Medicaid now, but I felt too abashed to ask.

Things went badly right from the start. I went into St. Vincent's in the middle of a heat wave, and the air conditioning in my room, with its permanently shut windows, was broken. I woke up after the operation in a sweat. Still delirious and in intense pain, I pulled off the stiff sheets to see that rather than the normal line of stitches I had expected along my hip, where they'd taken the graft, there was a long row of thirty or forty large metal staples. It looked as if someone had sawed my leg off and then put it back on with an office stapler. That sight upset me, but when I tried to speak, I found they'd given me a tracheotomy, another surprise.

Coming out of eight hours of anesthesia takes a long, unpleasant time. I kept surfacing into consciousness, taking note of one detail, such as the staples, then sinking back down again, only to reemerge a while later with no sense of how much time had passed, where I was, what on earth was happening. I couldn't understand why I had staples in my leg, and I was never coherent enough or conscious long enough to figure it out, to learn that it was simply an experiment in wound closure. I kept hallucinating gruesome scenes in which nurses were attacking me with pliers. My whole body kept shaking, and I found I could not stop crying, even though it did not feel as if I was the one crying: I was watching a movie of someone else lying in a bed, trembling and crying. I felt like a small child. I didn't feel safe.

At some point in the night I found it difficult to breathe. I wrote out a note to the nurse, who said she would tell the doctor. An hour later it was worse; I had to think about every breath. I wrote another note to the nurse, and finally a doctor arrived to draw an arterial blood sample to check my oxygen level. A long time went by. It was still dark, and there didn't seem to be any people around. I was frightened. When the doctor returned and started taking another blood sample, I was only dimly aware of him. I couldn't see very clearly, and his voice sounded muffled as he said hello to another doctor, who walked in and asked, "Didn't you just do a blood gas a little while ago?" I could hear them talking as if through water. "Yeah," he replied congenially, "but I didn't believe anyone's oxygen level could be that low." However unable I was to communicate with the outside world, this comment jolted my inside voice awake. Oh my God, I thought to myself, brain damage — I'm going to have brain damage, I'm going to be brain-dead, and as far as I could tell, no one seemed to care very much.

I lay in bed and focused on someone's hand resting on the end rail of my bed. Several people were having a conversation about what to do with me, but I couldn't concentrate on it. All I could think about was how cinematic this pale hand looked, resting there on its wrist and gracefully, limply, letting its fingers point toward the sheets. Sometimes it would twitch up, even turn its palm upward a little, as a hand would do when its owner was making a point. Then it was lifted up and taken away, and someone stepped up next to me and leaned down to tell me they were going to take me to Intensive Care, that I was going to be put on a respirator.

Now this, I thought, sounds like an excellent idea. Finally I'll be able to breathe. My few belongings were taken out of the bedside cabinet, put into a plastic bag, and plopped on the bed near my feet. The brakes were lifted off the bed's wheels, and off we went, me in a bed pushed by a nurse and a student doctor. The hospital seemed deserted, and we got lost twice, the nurse and student doctor arguing about which hallway to go down, blaming each other like an old married couple. Knowing there was a respirator in my future, I was a bit more relaxed and could see some comic aspects to my predicament.

After I was finally put on the respirator, it was discovered that I had pneumonia. I spent a hellish week in Intensive Care, where the lights were on twenty-four hours a day, the air conditioning was still broken, and every once in a while the alarm on my heart monitor would go off for no apparent reason. It was very loud and always jolted me right off the sheets. I had to wait for someone to come give it a whack, like a malfunctioning television, before it would stop.

The oddest part, though, was that everyone seemed to be speaking very peculiarly to me. I couldn't put my finger on what was so bizarre about their speech (was I on some strange drug?). Finally a male nurse I'd never seen before asked, very slowly and with overexaggerated movements of his mouth, "How long did it take you to learn lip reading?" For some inexplicable reason, they thought I was deaf. Later that day a crew of workmen started ripping down a wall a few feet from the foot of my bed in order to fix some pipes. Their jackhammers made my metal bed rails jingle and set my heart monitor off again.

While in the hospital I had been so ill that I hadn't put much effort into thinking about my appearance. My mother had been given the use of an apartment on the Upper East Side for the summer, and afterward I went to stay with her. One whole living room wall was covered with mirrors. I walked into the apartment and almost fainted at the sight of me. The graft had been applied not to just one side of my face but from one ear to the next and was obscenely swollen to the size of a football. A very large piece of pale skin from my hip had been left in, not just a small patch like the last time. This strip was a foot long and four inches wide, and on either side of it were long rows of sutures. If feeling like a freak had been more in my mind than in my face at other times in my life, the visage I saw staring back at me was undeniably repulsive. The feeling was confirmed for me whenever I went out on the street. People would stop in their tracks and stare at me. One afternoon a beggar ran up behind me, demanding money. I stopped and turned around to look at him. He stopped in midsentence, looked at me for a second longer, then politely apologized and handed me a dollar bill before turning away, muttering to himself. My self-esteem reached the bottom of the deepest, darkest pit.

I was promised a revision operation before going back

to school, and I placed all my hope on that. Maybe it wasn't really so bad after all, I tried to tell myself: the swelling would eventually go down and the skin would be taken away. I simply had to accept that and try my best to make use of the time spent waiting, numb any and all desires to look normal. I spent a lot of time sitting alone in the dark kitchen, which had only one small, lightless window, sweating from the heat and giving myself pep talks, diatribes on the truer meaning of life.

One afternoon the phone rang. It was Greg, one of my friends from college. When he asked how I was, I tried to answer, but all that came out was choking tears. "Hang on," he said, "I'm coming to get you." An hour later the bell rang. When I opened the door, I expected to have to go into a long explanation about why I looked the way I did, but before I could start Greg announced we were going dancing that night. Dancing? Was he serious? He was. He had only just come out as a homosexual, and he told me I was the only one he trusted enough to accompany him to the gay clubs. It was important, he said: he was counting on me to support him.

My own sexuality completely on hold, I found myself in a world composed of sex. I felt both safe and amazed by my sudden proximity to dozens of half-naked men suggestively grinding their hips on the dance floor. The club was called The Monster, and the sex here had nothing to do with me. No one took any notice of me — I was without value in this world. It was easy to sublimate my own desire and sustain my feelings of physical worthlessness. I put all my energy into learning to dance. My teachers were some of the great anonymous masters of the mid-eighties dance club scene. I spent my first few visits watching before finally getting up enough nerve to go out on the floor myself. Never in a million years would I have been able to do this in a heterosexual club, but here, what the hell? I learned the balance between letting loose and keeping control, allowing my body to react impulsively to the beat and directing that impulse into a more meditated, skilled movement. It was all about rhythm, about finding the place where the music's rhythm met my own. As I danced I thought how this wasn't all that different from making art. Every once in a while I would think, fleetingly, that this must also be what it was like to act sexually in the world. But mostly I just treated the experience academically.

Later, in my senior year, I became friends with a group of transvestites I'd met in the clubs. They took me under their wing. Lying back on a clothes-strewn bed, I'd spend long evenings watching them prepare to go out, a process that could last for hours. Their notions of beauty were extreme: gobs of makeup, technicolor dresses, and, most crucial of all, they tried to impress upon me, the art of accessorizing. Sometimes my friends would drag me off the bed and gather around to play with me, experimenting with different makeup techniques. They put on absurd amounts of everything from foundation to lipstick to false eyelashes. Looking at myself in the mirror, I was in little danger of having to think of myself as a "real" girl doing real girl things. I'd been trying for an androgynous effect, and with my slight figure shrouded in baggy clothes, I was often mistaken for a boy. I felt very safe dressed this way. As I watched my friends dress up, I felt very far away from my own femininity.

I relished the eccentrics in my life. I seemed to know a lot of them, and each one introduced me to others. A friend of a friend introduced me to Divine, the famous female impersonator, and I found myself at parties populated by the likes of Andy Warhol, famous fashion designers, erstwhile rock stars. They rarely gave me more than a passing glance, but I felt a strange sense of belonging within these crowds of people, all of us so excessively bound to the world of appearance. I went to all the hippest of the hip clubs and danced myself into a frenzy.

Walking around these dark clubs, I felt the same strange power I used to feel among the parents at the pony parties. As long as I disengaged any expectations of being physically desired by anyone, I was able to indulge a fantasy of myself as an artist, as someone special, a face you remembered.

The summer after my sophomore year came to an end, the grotesque swelling came down, and I had a revision operation. Though I didn't feel particularly good about my image, I didn't feel bad about it either. This was a momentous step forward, and I decided to push myself one step further. I cut my hair. I knew it was the only way I would ever stop hiding behind it. Starting off with a long bob, I worked in small stages, every few weeks making it shorter and shorter. By the end of my junior year it was only a few inches long. During that year the free flap was slowly reabsorbed, as the last one had been. Once again I had nothing to show for the operation but the scarred donor site. Finally, the summer before my final year at college, I was scheduled for a bone graft.

The graft would be nonvascularized, meaning a lump of bone would be taken from my hip, ground up, and then, like clay, fashioned into the rough shape of a jaw. The effects of this operation were immediately apparent and remarkable, because bone doesn't swell. I remember limping out of bed to the bathroom and not believing my own eyes as I swung open the door. Could that really be me? For weeks afterward I kept putting my hand up and checking to make sure it was still there, an actual jaw. For the first time in memory, I actually looked forward to seeing myself in the mirror, seeing a face I liked.

What puzzled me was that I still didn't feel attractive, despite what all my friends were telling me. Wasn't my fear just supposed to fall away, wasn't someone supposed to fall in love with me, wasn't life supposed to *work* now? Where was all that relief and freedom that I thought came with beauty?

TWELVE

Mirrors

⌐

THE GENERAL PLOT OF LIFE IS SOMETIMES SHAPED by the different ways genuine intelligence combines with equally genuine ignorance. I put all my effort into looking at the world as openly, unbiasedly, and honestly as possible, but I could not recognize my own self as a part of this world. I took great pains to infuse a sense of grace and meaning into everything I saw, but I could not apply those values to myself. Personally, I felt meaningless, or, more precisely, I felt I meant nothing to no one.

Even though I now possessed many rich friendships, had people who valued me, not having a lover meant I was ultimately unlovable. I didn't realize what a major step forward it was for me to begin to own my desires. But rather than finding affirmation in knowing my friends loved me, I turned it against myself: if so many people thought I was such a lovable person, the fact that I still wasn't able to get a lover proved I was too ugly. Whatever sense of inner worth I developed was eroded by the knowledge that I could only compensate for, but never over-come, the obstacle of my face.

I was consumed with self-pity, but try as I might I couldn't shake it. Because I had grown up denying myself any feeling that even hinted at self-pity, I now had to find a way to reshape it. Just as I had been comforted by the Christian pamphlets that came in the mail, I now read the Bible, though I could not find it within myself to believe. In the Old and New Testaments I recognized a certain movement of time, a cycle of mourning that began with expulsion and moved toward reconciliation. It was the dynamic of my own life, reaffirmed in a different lan-guage. I read various philosophers and imagined my soul, separate and clear of my heart and mind. At times I was so lonely I was amazed I didn't just expire right there on the spot, as if loneliness that strong were a divine thunderbolt that could strike me down at any moment, whether I was in bed, at a crowded dinner table, or at an empty roadside stop.

Not surprisingly, I saw sex as my salvation. If only I could get someone to have sex with me, it would mean that I was attractive, that someone could love me. I never doubted my own ability to love, only that the love would never be returned. The longing for someone and the fear that there would never be anyone intermingled to the point where I couldn't tell the difference. My longing itself, my neediness, transformed itself into a firm belief that my love would never be reciprocated. The major reason I was still a virgin when I graduated from college was obviously the lack of genuine opportunities combined with my crippling lack of self-esteem, but I persisted in seeing it as proof that I had lost out on the world of love only because of my looks.

All of this would change when I went to graduate school. Having long given up on the idea of going to medical school, I applied to MFA programs in poetry. If sex wasn't going to be my salvation, writing and poetry would be. But within two days of arriving at the University of Iowa, I met the man who would become my first lover. There was no doubt I was an easy mark. On the surface Jude was everything I imagined I wanted: an older, handsome writer who drove an antique sports car and had an unusual name and a quirky personality. He had lived a difficult, interesting life. On the whole he was, as he loved to hear me describe him, terribly dashing.

The relationship was a disaster. I never for a moment thought I was in love with Jude or that he was in love with me, but it was a highly charged sexual relationship. At last I had found a man who was attracted to me, and I allowed his attraction to define me. At his prompting, I began dressing more like "a woman," even though I still could not bring myself to use the personal pronoun and the word *woman* in the same sentence. At first I felt like an imposter, but as time wore on even I had to admit I had a sexy body. I went from looking like a boy to wearing miniskirts, garter belts, and high heels. Once I started dressing provocatively I couldn't stop. It was just as much a costume as dressing androgynously had been, and even though these new dresses hid none of my curves, I believed they hid my fear of being ugly. I thought I could use my body to distract people from my face. It made me feel worthy: I even got dressed up to go to the supermarket.

All of my parading around couldn't hide the fact that the bone graft was slowly going the way of the other grafts. I didn't really notice it until the day after Jude broke up with me. Looking in the mirror, I saw the telltale signs and felt a huge dread come over me. It had all been a lie. I had fooled Jude into thinking I was something other than what I was, and now reality was slowly, relentlessly manifesting itself again. This is when I began dressing in earnest slinkiness. I began spending two hours a day at the gym, imposing a killer regime on myself. My body was one thing I had control over. If I had put a tenth of the energy I spent obsessing over my face and my body into my work, I could have written *War and Peace* ten times over.

Bent on proving I was desirable, I started collecting lovers, having a series of short-term relationships that always ended, I was certain, because I wasn't beautiful enough. I became convinced that anyone who wanted to have a real relationship with me was automatically someone I didn't want. It was the classic Groucho Marx paradox: I didn't want to belong to any club that would have me as a member.

Dr. Baker and I decided to try another soft-tissue free flap. So much of the original irradiated tissue had been replaced with nonirradiated tissue that he felt there was a good chance this graft would stick. But a few months before the operation, I discovered that Medicaid would not pay my hospital bills. The accumulated reasons ranged from my not living in the state where the operation was to be performed to my being a full-time student with a teaching fellowship. I had to put off the operation until the following summer.

Dr. Baker suggested I go to the University of Iowa hospital for a consultation with the head of plastic surgery, who was an old friend of his. Perhaps there was a way for him to do the operation. Because Iowa's Medicaid system was on a first-come, first-serve funding basis, I could not apply for funding before the operation: I had to have it, submit the bills, and wait to see if there was enough left in the budget to pay for it. I wasn't very optimistic when I went for my appointment.

The surgeon was from the old school. Of course my free flaps had shrunk, he told me; they always did. He suggested sticking with the pedestal method that Dr. Conley had outlined for me so many years ago. He was very enthusiastic, explaining in far greater detail than Conley had about all the different incisions he'd make. He described how I could stay in the hospital for the six weeks when my hand was sewn to my stomach and then to my face; while my hand was sewn to my face he would rig up a special cast to hold everything in place. He even introduced me to a patient of his who was having a pedestal to rebuild his nose. This patient's nose had been shot off with a gun, and he was sporting a very complicated and uncomfortable-looking cast that was forcibly holding his wrist to his face. Connecting his wrist to the area of his nose was a pale tube of skin with a red row of sutures down the side. I felt totally repulsed, and ashamed of my repulsion.

After this patient had left, and not wanting to be rude, I calmly told the surgeon that I probably couldn't go through with the operations after all because of the money involved. "Oh, don't let that worry you. You wait right here." He disappeared for a long fifteen minutes, leaving me alone in the office. I decided this was as good a time as any to see if I could have an out-of-body experience. Having read only in passing about out-of-body experiences, and these mostly in supermarket tabloids, I thought you were supposed to follow an actual physical route, so I closed my eyes and tried imagining what the air duct over my head would look like if I were inside it.

Eventually the surgeon returned with a hospital financial officer, who outlined a payment plan for the three major operations and the minor follow-up, as well as the extended inpatient stays. When he had finished his calculations, he assured me that with payments of only a hundred dollars a month I could pay off the original bill and all the accumulated interest by the time I was forty-two. He was very affable, and I shook his hand, telling him I'd think about it.

I stayed calm until I reached the street, when I broke into a run and didn't stop until I got home, four miles away. There I started to hyperventilate. I was even more upset that my body should betray me now, just when I most needed it. There was no way I was going to put myself through those operations, let alone have the pleasure of paying them off just when I should be rightfully starting my midlife crisis along with everybody else.

There I was with my short skirts and sharp mind and

list of lovers, trying so hard to convince myself that maybe all I really needed to do was learn how to treat myself better. I was on the verge of learning this, yet I was still so suspicious, so certain that only another's love could prove my worth absolutely. Forget all that now, though, because here was the ugly truth. I felt I had been shown a mirror of what my life really was, what I really was, and I did not want to look. I was someone whom doctors talked to about sewing her hand to her face. I was trying to believe there really wasn't all that much wrong with me, but here were my worst suspicions, confirmed.

Lying in my usual abject heap on the living-room carpet, a pose I often adopted in dire times, I mouthed the words "I'm tired. I don't want to do this anymore." For once I didn't adopt either a noble or a catastrophic interpretation of events. I'd been so hell-bent on accepting everything that happened, on trying to inject some grand scheme of meaning, that the thought of simply rejecting everything felt akin to heresy. It was reality, after all: I did have cancer once, I did have a disfigured face now, there was no denying these two things. I felt pulled in two different directions. I had tasted what it was like to feel loved, to feel whole, and I had liked that taste. But fear kept insisting that I needed someone else's longing to believe in that love. No matter how philosophical my ideals, I boiled every equation down to these simple terms: was I lovable or was I ugly?

As radical a decision as it was to simply *not* try to reach a conclusion, I knew that one way or another I would have an operation. This, I felt, was beyond my control. After a great deal of finagling, I managed to find funding for the next free flap from a charity through the New York University Center for Reconstructive Surgery. Dr. Baker did the operation that summer, and it was the usual story of hope and disappointment. I looked horrendous for a few months, then I looked better, and just as I was getting used to the new face, the graft started disappearing. I thought about trying another bone graft, but when I discovered that there was a limit to the number of times I could apply for funds, I decided to give it up. This was me, this was my face, like it or lump it.

I opted for a geographic cure, deciding to go live in Europe once school was finished. I took on extra jobs, worked around the clock, and in a few months saved two thousand dollars and bought a ticket to Berlin. An old college friend was living there, which seemed as good a reason as any to pick that destination.

West Berlin, the Wall still intact at the time, fueled every romantic notion I had about living the bohemian life. I lived in a flat heated by giant prewar porcelain stoves, with no proper bathroom. Each morning I bathed in the kitchen sink. I applied for jobs teaching English at various schools and went to Kreuzberg, a poor, rundown area near the Wall, for very cheap German lessons, along with a room full of Turkish immigrants. While waiting to hear about jobs, I spent my days sitting in cafés, trying to write the ultimate poem about beauty and truth while simultaneously plotting to get rich from writing the great transatlantic trashy novel.

Living in a country where I didn't speak the language suited me just fine. Everything was an adventure, including buying milk at the corner store. I developed the art of getting lost. Intending to ride one U-Bahn line, I'd often end up in a completely different part of town, with only my own wits and the help of strangers to get me back home. It was a safe kind of chaos, and at some point I understood that I was cultivating my "aloneness" in this strange place as a method for putting off loneliness.

I maintained a romantic picture of myself as an expat artist in Berlin for as long as possible, until all my job possibilities fell through. Running low on funds, I decided to go to London and live with my sister Susie. I figured I'd find work more readily in a country where I spoke the language.

Usually cities offered me the refuge of anonymity, but everything felt different in London. Though I'd toned down my fashion sense quite a bit since Iowa, I still enjoyed wearing clothes that showed off my figure. Groups of men, mostly young and drunk, would spot me from a distance and follow me, catcalling. It was like junior high school all over again. As soon as they got near enough to see my face clearly, they'd start teasing me, calling me ugly, thinking it hysterically funny to challenge one another to ask me out on a date. I always stayed calm, kept right on walking, keeping my composure, but it was exhausting. I knew it had to do with their being drunk, that they would have targeted anyone in their path, that I just happened to be in the wrong place at the wrong time, but none of this helped.

One evening, after I'd come home visibly upset from some teasing, my sister mentioned a surgeon named Oliver Fenton. While I was in Iowa, just after my last failed free flap, she'd read about a new method for plastic surgery he was working on, known as a tissue expander. She had written to him and asked whether this new procedure might be of any benefit to me. He called her back himself and told her he thought it might work. When she had called me from London, I was very doubtful.

People were always telling me about the "wonderful things they can do today." It was difficult explaining to them — even apologizing for the fact — that plastic surgery wasn't like the movies. There was never a dramatic moment when the bandages came off, nor a single procedure that would make it all right. As soon as my sister told me about this new doctor, I forgot all about him. Now she mentioned him again, how nice he'd sounded on the phone, how it couldn't hurt to at least go see him. He lived in Aberdeen, Scotland, seven hours by train from London. I couldn't afford the train ticket, and in all likelihood I would have skipped it if Susie hadn't generously offered to buy the ticket as a present.

Fenton explained the whole procedure to me. First he would insert a tissue expander, to be followed by a vascularized bone graft. Because the bone graft would have its own blood supply, the chances of it being reabsorbed were minimal. The procedure would take at least six months to finish; I knew enough about plastic surgery by then to know this probably meant a year. Telling him I'd think about it, I boarded the train back to London. In the dining car I encountered yet another pack of drunken men more than willing to judge my looks for me.

I was frightened that none of Fenton's proposed operations would work, that I would only be letting myself in again for that familiar disappointment. But, again but, how could I pass up the possibility that it might work, that at long last I might finally fix my face, fix my life, my soul? And thanks to my Irish passport and socialized medicine, the operations would be free. Remembering the drunken but nonetheless cruel comments of those men on the train, I called up the doctor and told him yes.

An empty balloon was inserted under the skin on the right side of my face and then slowly blown up by daily injections of a few milliliters of saline salution into a special port beside my ear. The objective was to slowly stretch out the skin, much the way a pregnancy stretches the belly, so that there would be enough of my own skin to pull down and cover the bone graft. The whole process took about three months, and I spent the entire time in the hospital. All in all, I had a great time.

The others on the ward took it upon themselves to teach me about Scotland. The dialect was almost impenetrable at first, but I wasn't half bad at understanding it by the time I left. Certain patients became my good friends, and after they were released, they took me for day trips to the beautiful countryside surrounding the city. The landscape brought up long-distant memories of Ireland. One of the doctors, a German woman named Eva, commiserated with me on our shared foreignness and invited me home with her sometimes after work to enjoy a good meal, which made me feel special, not like just another patient.

I was happy to be in the hospital, relieved not to have to go out into the world looking this way. My face transformed on a daily basis into something rather monstrous. It was beginning to look as if a big balloon had been put in my face. I knew my appearance was strange, but there were other people on the ward with tissue expanders, people worse off than myself, and I never felt the need to explain or apologize or feel ashamed of my appearance. Since physically I was capable of taking care of myself, and medically there was no need for me to be an inpatient, it did not escape my attention that I was being treated like a sick person simply because I did not look like other people.

The big day finally came, and in what turned out to be an almost thirteen-hour operation, due to some minor unforeseen difficulties, the tissue expander was removed and the graft from my hip put in. I was severely disoriented when I woke up, a feeling exacerbated by the morphine they were giving me. The morphine didn't actually lessen the pain; rather, it diminished my scope of awareness. As I kept waking and sinking back under, I was overtaken by a brutal paranoia, convinced that because I had chosen to do this to myself, I deserved everything I got. Such long operations are rare, and I don't think the staff was aware of this side effect. I was a complete wreck, and no one knew how to reassure me. It wasn't until Susie came up from

London a couple of days later to visit me that the paranoia began to wear off. I don't think I'd ever been so happy to see someone in all my life.

Because of the bone taken from my hip, I was very lame for a long time. I tried not to think about the results. There were more revision operations to come, and I patiently waited for each of them. After a few, my face was beginning to look acceptable to me; the new graft was solid and didn't seem to be in jeopardy. But then something unexpected happened: the original bone on the left side of my jaw, which had also been heavily irradiated, was starting to shrink, probably spurred by the stress of such a large operation. The doctor proposed putting a tissue expander in on the left side, followed by yet another free flap.

I could not imagine going through it *again*, and just as I'd done all my life, I searched and searched for a way to make it okay, make it bearable, for a way to *do* it. I lay awake all night on the train back to London. I realized then that I had no obligation to improve my situation, that I didn't have to explain or understand my life, that I could simply let it happen. By the time the train pulled into King's Cross Station I felt able to bear it yet again, not entirely sure what other choice I had.

I moved to Scotland, partly to be near the hospital and partly because I wanted more independence. Eligible for social security benefits, I was able to get my own, albeit very cold, flat overlooking a bridge under which whores congregated at night.

When I arrived at the hospital to set up a date to have the tissue expander inserted, I was informed that I would

spend only three or four days there after the initial procedure. Almost in a whisper, I asked if I would be staying in
the hospital for the three months of expansion time. No
— instead I was to come in every day to the outpatient
ward. Horrified by this prospect, I left there speechless. I
would have to live and move about in the outside world
for three months with a giant balloon stuck in my face. In
the few days before I went into the hospital I spent a great
deal of time drinking alone, both in bars and at home. I
even picked up a man, a sweet and handsome man, probably every bit as lonely as I was. Lying next to him after it
was over, I remember thinking I was fooling him, that he
didn't have any idea who, or what, he was really with.

I went into the hospital, had the operation, and went
home at the end of the week. The only things that gave
me any comfort during the months I lived with my face
gradually ballooning out were my writing and my reading.
I wrote for hours and hours each day and lost myself
reading everything from Kafka to Jackie Collins. I'd usually walk to the hospital, even though it was several miles,
because I didn't want to get on the bus and feel trapped
that way. Luckily it was also cold, so I could wrap my
whole head in a scarf. As the tissue expander grew and
grew, this became harder to do. I stopped going out except
to the hospital and to the little store around the corner
from me to buy food. I knew the people who worked
there, and I kept wondering when they were going to ask
what was wrong. I assumed they thought I had some
massive tumor and were afraid to ask.

Finally I couldn't stand the polite silence any longer. I

blurted out my whole life story to the man behind the counter. I was holding a glass bottle of milk, letting the whole saga stream out of me, when the bells tied to the door jangled. The man who walked in was completely covered with tattoos. I stopped in midsentence and stared at him. He stopped in midstride and stared at me. There was a puma reaching across his cheek toward his nose, which had some kind of tree on it, the trunk of it running along the bridge, then flowering up on his forehead. He hadn't even one inch of naturally colored skin: his ears, neck, and hands were covered with lush jungle scenes and half-naked women with seashells covering their breasts.

I don't know why, but I felt immensely sorry for him. We finally broke our mutual stares, I paid for my milk, he bought a pack of cigarettes, and we walked out together, turning different ways at the corner. In the same way that imagining living in Cambodia had helped me as a child, I walked the streets of my dark little Scottish city by the sea and knew without doubt that I was living in a story Kafka would have been proud to write.

The one good thing about a tissue expander is that you look so bad with it in that no matter what you look like when it's finally removed, it has to be better. I had the graft and some revision operations, and by that summer, yes, even I had to admit I looked better. But I didn't look like me. Something was wrong: was *this* the face I had waited for through eighteen years and almost thirty operations? I couldn't make what I saw in the mirror correspond to the person I thought I was. It wasn't only that I continued to feel ugly; I simply could not conceive of the image as belonging to me. I had known this feeling before, but that had been when my face was "unfinished," when I still had a large gap where my jaw should have been. I'd been through twelve operations in the three years I'd been living in Scotland: Fenton was running out of things to do to me. There were still some minor operations, but for the most part it was over. Was this it? How could this be? Even as people confirmed that this was now my face, even as people congratulated me, I felt I was being mistaken for someone else. The person in the mirror was an imposter — why couldn't anyone else see this?

The only solution I could think of was to stop looking. It wasn't easy. I'd never suspected just how omnipresent our own images are. I became an expert on the reflected image, its numerous tricks and wiles, how it can spring up at you at any moment from a glass tabletop, a well-polished door handle, a darkened window, a pair of sunglasses, a restaurant's otherwise magnificent brass-plated coffee machine sitting innocently by the cash register. I perfected the technique of brushing my teeth without a mirror, grew my hair in such a way that it would require only a quick, simple brush, and wore clothes that were easily put on, with no complex layers or lines that might require even a minor visual adjustment. I did this for almost a year.

The journey back to my face was a long one. Between operations, thanks to some unexpected money inherited from my grandmother, I traveled around Europe. I kept writing. I returned to Berlin and sat in the same cafés as before, but now without my image, without the framework of *when my face gets fixed, then I'll start living.* I felt there was something empty about me. I didn't tell anyone, not my sister, not my closest friends, that I had stopped looking in mirrors. I found that I could stare straight through a mirror, allowing none of the reflection to get back to me.

Unlike some stroke victims, who are physically unable to name the person in the mirror as themselves, my trick of the eye was the result of my lifelong refusal to learn *how* to name the person in the mirror. My face had been changing for so long that I had never had time to become acquainted with it, to develop anything other than an ephemeral relationship with it. It was easy for me to ascribe to physical beauty certain qualities that I thought I simply had to wait for. It was easier to think that I was still not beautiful enough or lovable enough than to admit that perhaps these qualities did not really belong to this thing I thought was called beauty after all.

Without another operation to hang all my hopes on, I was completely on my own. And now something inside me started to miss me. A part of me, one that had always been there, organically *knew* I was whole. It was as if this part had known it was necessary to wait so long, to wait until the impatient din around it had quieted down, until the other internal voices had grown exhausted and hoarse before it could begin to speak, before I would begin to listen.

*   *   *

One evening near the end of my long separation from the mirror, I was sitting in a café talking to a man I found quite attractive when I suddenly wondered what I looked like to him. What was he actually *seeing* in me? I asked myself this old question, and startlingly, for the first time in my life, I had no ready answer. I had not looked in a mirror for so long that I had no idea what I objectively looked like. I studied the man as he spoke; for all those years I'd handed my ugliness over to people and seen only the different ways it was reflected back to me. As reluctant as I was to admit it now, the only indication in my companion's behavior was positive.

And then I experienced a moment of the freedom I'd been practicing for behind my Halloween mask all those years ago. As a child I had expected my liberation to come from getting a new face to put on, but now I saw it came from shedding something, shedding my image.

I used to think truth was eternal, that once I *knew*, once I *saw*, it would be with me forever, a constant by which everything else could be measured. I know now that this isn't so, that most truths are inherently unretainable, that we have to work hard all our lives to remember the most basic things. Society is no help. It tells us again and again that we can most be ourselves by acting and looking like someone else, only to leave our original faces behind to turn into ghosts that will inevitably resent and haunt us. As I sat there in the café, it suddenly occurred to me that it is no mistake when sometimes in films and literature the dead know they are dead only after being offered that most irrefutable proof: they can no longer see themselves in the mirror.

Feeling the warmth of the cup against my palm, I felt this small observation as a great revelation. I wanted to tell the man I was with about it, but he was involved in his own thoughts and I did not want to interrupt him, so instead I looked with curiosity at the window behind him, its night-silvered glass reflecting the entire café, to see if I could, now, recognize myself.

ACKNOWLEDGMENTS

I would like to thank the Bunting Institute of Radcliffe
College, the Corporation of Yaddo, and the Fine Arts
Work Center in Provincetown.

Afterword

⌐

NOW THERE IS A SECOND ENDING TO THIS STORY. LUCY Grealy died on December 18, 2002. She was thirty-nine years old. Many people have asked me if she died of cancer, and even though she had been free of cancer since she was ten, there is a sense in which that disease and its aftermath were a large part of what killed her. She continued to struggle all her life with the issues she wrote about here: reconstructive surgeries, loneliness, and the pain of feeling different. Some people, having read this book, will say her life was simply too hard. Her life was hard, but it was also filled with incredible joy. One of her greatest joys was the publication of this book.

In the fall of 1994 it was clear to everyone that *Autobiography of a Face* was turning out to be a huge critical and commercial success. At the same time it was becoming clear that my just published second novel, *Taft*, was going to vanish without a trace. When I was scheduled to give a reading in New York, Lucy suggested that we team up, appear as a double bill, and then afterward she would throw us a big book party at her Soho loft. She was my best friend, and she was lending me the brilliance of her light in a moment when things were looking decidedly dull for me. It was something we did for each other over the years, depending on which of us had more light to share at the moment. At the beautiful and now departed downtown Rizzoli's, the dozen or so Ann Patchett fans squeezed in among the Lucy Grealy throng of well over two hundred. Not that anyone was keeping score. The manager tucked us upstairs, away from the crowd, so that we could make a sweeping entrance. We hid together between some bookshelves and listened to the buzz of voices, laughing to think they were all waiting for us. Lucy was famous, and I was famous for being with her.

There was a lot of cancer in the room that night,

cancer in the process of being defeated and cancer in the process of defeating people. There were the ravages that cancer, long gone, had left in its wake, including the damage it had done to Lucy. It was not a crowd who had come to hear fiction, any fiction, and I told Lucy I was going to go first. I was the warm-up act. I read for five minutes, answered two questions, and got back in my seat so that I could see the show we had all come for.

As Lucy quickly discovered, the problem with writing a memoir was that once people had read her story they thought they knew her. They filled in any parts that may be missing with details from their own lives, thus creating a picture in which the author and the reader are intertwined. But I did know Lucy. We had gone to college together. We had lived together in Iowa while we went to graduate school. We had worn each other's clothes, read our favorite books aloud, spent each other's money, and often ate off the same plate. Once when we were in graduate school a film crew came from Ireland to do a documentary on her. "It's going to be about the triumph of the human spirit," the producer said. But Lucy couldn't pull herself together for the shoot. She couldn't stop laughing. The last thing she saw herself as, the last thing she wanted to be, was the poster girl for the human spirit. A week later we were sitting together in a lecture on Faulkner and I passed Lucy a slip of paper with the single word "triumph" written on it. She started laughing, and this time she simply could not stop. She became so hysterical that finally, red-faced with tears pouring down her cheeks, she had to excuse herself from class.

As the crowd in Rizzoli's wept over the passage she read about being tortured by schoolboys in stairwells, my brave and heroic Lucy made it clear to the audience that she had no interest in being anybody's inspiration. She was not there as a role model for overcoming obstacles. She was a serious writer, and she wanted her book to be judged for its literary merit and not its heartbreaking content. When people raised their hand to ask a question, more often than not that question turned out to be a statement of what they themselves had endured. Lucy refused to let the evening digress into a litany of battle stories.

"Most of the time I forget I even had cancer," Lucy said. "That's not the part of the story I'm interested in."

"When I got my own diagnosis," a woman started,

and Lucy listened with moderate patience. When the speaker was finished, Lucy only nodded and pointed to the next hand that was raised.

"It's amazing how you remember everything so clearly," a woman said, her head wrapped in a bright scarf. "All those conversations, details. Were you ever worried that you might get something wrong?"

"I didn't remember it," Lucy said pointedly. "I wrote it. I'm a writer."

This shocked the audience more than her dismissal of illness, but she made her point: she was making art, not documenting an event. That she chose to tell her own extraordinary story was of secondary importance. Her cancer and subsequent suffering had not made this book. She had made it. Her intellect and ability were in every sense larger than the disease.

By telling us that the sentences spoken in the book were not necessarily verbatim, Lucy claimed complete ownership of her history. It was her world and she would present it the way she wanted to. Her memory and desire were indeed the facts. She taught me something while I sat in the audience that night about the nature of writing and the nature of truth. In the right hands, a memoir is the flecks of gold panned out of a great, muddy river. A memoir is those flecks melted down into a shapable liquid that can then be molded and hammered into a single bright band to be worn on a finger, something you could point to and say, "This? Oh, this is my life." Everyone has a muddy river, but very few have the vision, patience, and talent to turn it into something so beautiful. This is why the writer matters, so that we can not only learn from her experience but find a way to shape our own. I'm not talking about shaping every life into a work of art, I'm talking about making our life into something we can understand, a portable object that contains the weight and power of an entire terrain.

Certainly, *Autobiography of a Face* can be read as an account of a child's cancer and disfigurement (a word Lucy despised), but it can also be read as it was written: as a piece of literature. Through the beauty of her language and the complexity of her reasoning, it ceases to be merely Lucy's sad story (if the word "merely" can be applied to such a story). Instead, she uses her own life as the step up to something universal. This is a book that understands how none of us

ever feel we are pretty enough while it makes us question the very concept of beauty. It touches on our
fears that love and approval are things we will always
have to struggle to keep. It takes something so personal and so horrible that it is, for most of us, completely beyond our comprehension, and turns it into
a mirror on ourselves. Lucy wanted people to relate to
her story, but not only on the level of physical suffering. She expected so much more of herself that she in
turn felt entitled to expect more of her readers. She
wanted us to learn not only about the facts but also
about their abstraction, to think beyond what we
already know. Lucy often talked about her mother's
theory how being brave and acting brave were essentially the same thing. Her mother would tell her that
if she felt terrified going into chemotherapy to simply
fake bravery and she would have excellent results. "If
I see someone drowning in a river and I don't feel
brave enough to jump in and save them, then I can
fake the bravery, which means I will still jump in and
save them," Lucy would tell me. The outcome is all
the same: the potential victim is rescued, and the
coward is a hero.

We would often joke that at the end of her life, an

event which we thought of as a long way off in the future, Lucy would write a sequel to this book called *Autobiography of a Face: The "Real" Story*. In this version, she would tell things absolutely as they happened, complete with all the sadness and pain and blame she had sidestepped in the first edition. One of the many remarkable things about the book she wrote is how much she chose to spare us. A true story, a story based on real life, can never be written completely, anymore than an entire river can be carried in your hand. Lucy knew she had to pick and choose her details because if she tried to tell them all, the reader would be crushed beneath their weight. She knew there was a good chance the rest of us lacked her bravery.

If I made a list of the things I personally miss about Lucy, and then added the things that we have all lost by not having her here in this world, the list would be longer than this book. I want more of everything where she is concerned: more of her time, more of her enormous capacity for joy, her dancing, her strong opinions about everything (especially politics and art), her generous and all-encompassing love, but right now, reading this book, I mostly wish

I had more of her writing. Read this book twice, and then read it again later. It will take that much time before you can get past what she went through and come to see the perfection of her sentences. In most ways Lucy had all the ideal elements of a writer: a mastery of language, a poet's touch, a million impassioned ideas, and a strong desire to be heard. What she was bad at was being alone. Lucy wanted the people she loved pressed up against her, with a secondary ring of people she had yet to meet but would surely want to know waiting in reserve. If no one called to interrupt her while she was working, she would pick up the phone and create the interruption herself, "Would you like to go for coffee?" If there was no one to have coffee with she would simply pack up her notebook computer and spend the day sitting in a coffee shop trying to write. She needed to feel the world brushing past her. She wanted the love and warmth of company even more than she wanted a shelf full of books with her name on the spine, which is saying something, because she wanted those books a lot.

But if we have to make due with a small body of work in which *Autobiography of a Face* is the jewel in the crown, then we still have a great deal. In the future, I will think of it as a circular book, a story whose ending always folds back around to the first page, where I can start it all over again.

The last time I talked to Lucy was a few days before her death. She was living with a friend in Connecticut then but was making plans to move back to the city. I told her to put it off. She had been through too much in the last year, in the last month, and she needed to rest and get stronger. She ignored me, of course. She said that she missed her friends, that she had to be back in New York. She told me she loved me and missed me and I told her the same. Ten seconds after I hung up, the phone rang again.

"You think I have talent, don't you?" she said.

"Absolutely."

"Okay," she said. "That's all." And then she hung up. She was gone.

I want the chance to say it again. Absolutely.

—Ann Patchett
February 2003